LETTERS HOME

First published in 2009 by

WOODFIELD PUBLISHING LTD
Bognor Regis ~ West Sussex ~ England ~ PO21 5EL
www.woodfieldpublishing.com

© Edmund Hodges, 2009

All rights reserved.
No part of this publication may be reproduced
or transmitted in any form or by any means,
electronic or mechanical, nor may it be stored
in any information storage and retrieval system,
without prior permission from the publisher.

The right of Edmund Hodges
to be identified as Author of this work
has been asserted in accordance with
the Copyright, Designs and Patents Act 1988

ISBN 1-84683-072-9

Letters Home

A National Serviceman's Sketchbook

Edmund Hodges

Woodfield

Woodfield Publishing Ltd
Woodfield House ~ Babsham Lane ~ Bognor Regis ~ West Sussex ~ PO21 5EL
telephone 01243 821234 ~ **e-mail** enquiries@woodfieldpublishing.co.uk

Interesting and informative books on a wide variety of subjects

For details of all our published titles visit our website at **www.woodfieldpublishing.co.uk**

*Selected passages from a total of 172 letters
sent home between March 1955 and July 1956
Illustrated with pages from the Author's sketchbooks*

The Author with Sphinx ~ Giza 1955

~ CONTENTS ~

Introduction v

On the Troopship 'Dilwara' – 8th March 1955 1
On board the 'Dilwara' – Thursday 10th March 1955...2
On the 'Dilwara' – Saturday evening March 12th 1955 5
Fayid, Egypt, Monday March 14th 1955 5
Fayid, in the cool of eve, Monday 14th March 6
Fayid, Sunday 27th March 1955 9
Fayid, Saturday 2nd April 1955 10
Fayid, April 12th 1955 10
Fayid, 23rd June 1955 15
Fayid, 1st July 1955 15
Fayid, Sunday 3rd July 1955 16
Fayid, Friday 15th July 1955 – 12 months done! 17
Fayid, 22nd July 1955 17
Fayid, 23rd July 1955 – Ismailia 18
Fayid, Friday 29th July 1955 20

Fayid, 20th August 1955 21

Fayid, 5th September 1955 22

5th November 1955 Episkopi – 3 GHQ move from Fayid, Egypt, to Episkopi, Cyprus 26

Episkopi, 15th November 1955 31

Episkopi, 23rd November 1955 32

Episkopi, 24th November 1955 33

Episkopi, 29th November 1955 34

Episkopi, 13th December 1955 35

Episkopi, Christmas 1955 35

Tea, Christmas Eve, 1955 36

Midnight Mass, Christmas 1955..37

Boxing Day 1955 40

Episkopi, 14th January 1956 40

Episkopi, 23rd January 1956 41

Episkopi, 7th February 1956 43

Episkopi, 9th February 1956 44

Episkopi, 14th February 1956..45

Episkopi, 17th February 1956..46

Episkopi, 21st February 1956..46

Episkopi, 24th February 1956..47

RAF Camp, Amman, Hashemite Kingdom of Jordan, Sunday 26th February 1956 48

Casa Nova Hostal, Old City, Jerusalem, 27th February 1956 52
Casa Nova Hostal, Old City, Jerusalem, 28th February, 1956 53
Casa Nova Hostal, Old City, Jerusalem, 1st March 1956 55
Casa Nova Hostal, Old City, Jerusalem, Friday 2nd March 1956 57
Casa Nova Hostal, Old City, Jerusalem, Saturday 3rd March 1956 59
Casa Nova Hostal, Old City, Jerusalem, Sunday 4TH March 1956 61
Tourist Hotel, Beirut, Lebanon, Monday 5th March 1956 62
Waynes Keep Transit Camp, Nicosia, Wednesday 7th March 1956 64
Waynes Keep Transit Camp, Nicosia, Wednesday 7th March 1956 65
Episkopi, Wednesday 7th March 1956 66
Episkopi, 25th March 1956 67
Episkopi, 4th April 1956 67
Episkopi, 10th April 1956 67
Episkopi, 29th April 1956 68
Episkopi, 30th April, 1956 70
Episkopi, 4th May 1956 70
Episkopi, 11th May 1956 71
Episkopi, 23rd May 1956 71
Episkopi, Friday 25th May 1956 72
Episkopi, 28th May 1956 75
Episkopi, 14th June 1956 75

Letters Home ~ iii

Episkopi, 18th June 1956 76
Episkopi, 27th June 1956 76
Episkopi, 3rd July 1956 77
Nicosia Transit Camp, 6th July 1956 78
P.S. added at Nicosia Airport, 7th July 1956 78

Introduction

23051232 Signalman Hodges, E.J. was three years older than most of his Call-up Group, 54-14, having been deferred to complete his Art studies for N.D.D. in Sculpture and Lettercutting.

He declined the offer of Officer Training and, after Basic and Teleprinter Training, was shipped out to Egypt and Cyprus.

The British Army was about to pull out of the Suez Canal Zone , the Suez War came two years later, and EOKA, under Colonel Grivas, was making life difficult in Cyprus.

He carried his Pay Book and a pocket sketchbook at all times and with his drawings, watercolour sketches and word pictures he fought against the "creative constipation" induced by Army life.

Visually excited by new surroundings, and wishing to express and share this, he wrote long letters home, and these letters were kept by his parents.

Some fifty years later, these jottings evoke a picture of experiences which would be impossible today due to wars and political developments, not to mention the advances in military communication and living conditions.

They are the reactions and observations of a young man adjusting to an alien way of life, resigned to the compulsory military interruption of his studies, somewhat contemptuous of military thinking, but making the best of the situation.

His promotion to Lance Corporal and detailing as Chief ZDK Clerk and 2 i/c Traffic Hall Supervisor indicate a serious dedication to the job in hand, which he carried through to his later career in Teaching.

His childhood had been disrupted by evacuation to three different parts of this country. Of his first 14 years, seven were wartime ones. His detachment and observant nature may have been fostered by this, together with the creative talent which led him to Art studies.

With 'O' Level French from school, he was teaching himself Spanish when called up.

His first visit, a year before National Service, to a mountain village in Mallorca, inspired a love for the Mediterranean light and an appetite for the sights, tastes and smells of the region.

Edmund Hodges
January 2009

The Author ~ sketching at Bir Odebe ~ Egypt 1955.

On the Troopship 'Dilwara' – 8th March 1955

We have just left Gibraltar behind us after a short and most enjoyable visit. Our passes allowed us two hours but I got back half an hour early and did a couple of very quick drawings from the deck. While I did so the Royal Yacht arrived for the Duke's visit.

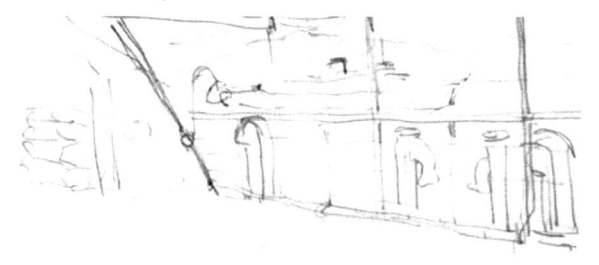

The Royal Yacht.

We cruised along some way off the Spanish coast and saw the snow capped range behind Malaga right up to nightfall. This morning we are out of sight of Spain but we can still see Africa and at mid day were on or near the Greenwich Line 0.

We may see the coast about Algiers before dark, then over to the Sicilian coast on the way down to Malta, where we hope to go ashore again.

Gibraltar reminded me very much of Palma, but of course it is much more up and down. The whole place is so Spanish, but all the goods in the shops seemed the same as at home. Election notices were in Spanish. I found the Cathedral near the Post Office. It is quite small and mostly obstructed by large piers.

Gibraltar harbour.

We started "school" on board this morning and I found I was landed with the job of assistant to a Mrs. Wilson in charge of the five to seven year olds! Fortunately she displayed considerable experience and invention and ran things while I supplied and collected chalks, pencils and paper and generally kept an eye on things in the background. Very interesting to watch. I may even be able to draw the children while they're otherwise occupied by a story or something.

In two hours they went through a period each of drawing, writing their names, being engines and rubber balls (!), resting while eating a sweet, and counting and drawing numbers and groups of things, and then stories and rhymes.

This afternoon they're to have a film show so that should be no trouble at all.

The rock.

On board the 'Dilwara' – Thursday 10th March 1955

Today has really been Malta day. First thing this morning I came up on deck and saw land just visible ahead. This turned out to be a sizeable island and as we got closer it became more and more like a fairy tale picture. The coast was alternately sharp cliffs and grassy slopes to the sea. On the flat hill tops we could soon see three towns spreading themselves, each with a church rising clear of the other buildings and forming a central point to each town.

We cruised along this coast for some long time, actually thinking it Malta, but at last we could see that a gap was appearing which separated this part from the land beyond. It was the island of Gozo, and soon after passing it we sighted a really big mass of buildings – Valetta.

As we drew near to this we were called to form up in three ranks facing the island to be inspected before proceeding ashore, and I must say not many Parades have had such a wonderful view!

Troopship 'Dilwara' moored in Valetta harbour.

Our Passes were then handed out and we were free to wander about the deck as the ship made her way between the breakwaters into the small harbour.

On each side were cool grey warships of the Royal Navy which contrasted wonderfully with the golden rock buildings which piled up to dizzy heights on all sides and were here and there topped by a variety of red domes on the churches.

This red colour was rather like that you get on those hard shiny patches on bricks that have been fired at a great heat, and was the only strong colour to set off the golden buildings.

At last we made fast to a buoy next to HMS *Jamaica* and we were ready to go ashore in the row boats coming out from the steps on the waterfront – ten of us in each.

Very elegant boats indeed, with scroll decoration painted in a band below the curving top and the strange uprights at each end of polished wood. I managed to get into the third boat and was soon ashore. We walked along the road by the quay side to the Barraca lift which took us up to the main town level.

From here the views across the harbour are really superb. Then we split up and made our way into Valetta itself. I found my way to the Cathedral, but it was shut.

Letters Home ~ 3

To judge from post cards it is highly decorated inside. Most streets shoot up and down at all angles and going was very difficult in steel shod boots.

All the churches I found were shut, but a Jewish friend remarked later (surprised) that he came across one which was open and packed, at 11.30 am! Many street corners have statues of the Madonna and Child and various saints, some life size, built into the corner of the wall.

Nearly everyone seems to have preferred Gibraltar to Malta, perhaps it is so much bigger they had to walk further to get as many shops in, and no one could get much idea of the place in a few hours. I can enjoy stone buildings in Mediterranean sunlight at any opportunity so the shops weren't what I judged the attraction of the place by.

We all had to be back on board at 3 pm and the ship sailed soon after. There was much shouting and banter as we passed each of the warships on the way out and everyone rushing from one rail to the other as we passed between them.

The beacon at the end of the breakwater is a lovely structure of yellowish-white stone, round in section and curving in and up like a vase with a small cornice on top and a thin iron lamp holder stuck on top rather oddly. The breakwater thickens and rises in a protective curve about the base of the tower.

Outside we were greeted by a destroyer which flashed a lamp and hoisted flags to us but we couldn't see any response from our bridge.

So, out again on our last lap, with Malta going down behind us with the sun.

Valetta.

On the 'Dilwara' – Saturday evening March 12th 1955

At last this happy respite has reached its end and we berth at Port Said at 1400 hrs tomorrow.

We go ashore in full "cold weather dress" with large packs on our backs, small packs slung over one shoulder, and carrying two kit-bags each – should be cosy!

Today we really sampled the heat to come and can only imagine the effect of losing our sea breezes. I don't mind heat but it feels so itchy about the waist with a BD and web belt.

Orders tonight state, among other things, collars and ties will be worn, no one will trade with the bum-boat traders alongside, no one will throw missiles at them!

Fayid, Egypt, Monday March 14th 1955

Well, here I am at last in 3 GHQ Signals at Fayid, a village of tents and sand and my, is this place f-l-a-t!

We got off the ship at Port Said, (more of that later), at about 4 pm and were loaded into trucks bound for our various units and camps and my party set off on the seventy odd mile ride to here. Along the Canal, then off into the barren sand dunes along a rather good Macadam roadway.

Many thanks for the letter I found waiting for me here.

It was dark and rather cold when we got in, and after issuing bedding and plates they gave us a meal and most of us went to bed in a marquee for a few nights until they sort us out into four-man tents.

Sufficient to say the camp itself is primitive in the extreme and its main advantage is that spit and polish is impossible – boots become dusty the moment you step into the sand.

All lorries leaving the camp carry escorts armed with Stens and the guards about the camp are armed too.

Letters Home ~ 5

At this end of the country we actually have a mountain visible to the west, and the Bitter Lake lies ten minutes walk away, very salty but good for a swim, I'm told.

The natives are the last word in primitives and we passed through several of their villages, looking just like the morning after the last night of a fairground, dusty, dirty, and all the huts in an apparent state of being stuck up or taken down, huts, tents, shacks and straw or oil drum enclosures.

Dust.

Fayid tents.

Fayid, in the cool of eve, Monday 14th March

Here to expand on the note of this morning.

We sighted land at 11.30 am Sunday morning – the mouth of the Nile, a long flat line broken by chimneys, cranes and a few tall buildings and rows of palms.

We anchored with a lot of other ships awaiting Pilots some way off shore. The Pilot came aboard from a little motor launch sent from the tug-like Pilot boat. Up anchor – and we zig-zagged at top speed along a path marked by buoys until we entered a straight channel marked at one side by a long breakwater of huge square blocks heaped on one another in a jagged pile. This became a solid wall and led to the shore, where a line of fishing boats were tied to it, by the famous statue of de Lesseps pointing into the Canal and on to the eastern waters beyond.

The buildings rising behind three solid rows of bathing huts on the beach were a mass of pale pink and browns, arcaded and pinnacled and set off by an occasional white one. Many carried neon lights advertising Craven A, Johnny Walker, etc.

6 ~ *Letters Home*

Fayid reception.

Passing a small boat, from which two men leaned on either side, one washing his feet, the other drinking with his hand as a scoop, we came to a widened part of the channel where large oil tanks labelled 'Esso' in English and Arabic stood on one side of a corner shaped quay.

Here we dropped anchor and were pulled by tugs so that our stern was in the corner. Then a pontoon walkway was pushed out to the ship and the ladderways lowered.

Meanwhile we had been issued with Egyptian money and a mob of "wogs" had come aboard to unload the boxes from the hold, slyly offering watches and jewellery to us when we were anywhere out of sight of the bridge. No takers.

When the families had gone ashore it was our turn and we staggered in full BD carrying two kit bags and large and small packs down a narrow stair, along a deck, down a shaky Jacob's ladder onto the swaying pontoon, along about 120 yards to collapse in three ranks on the quayside.

Here we waited some time before our open-sided canvas-topped trucks came for us, each with its two Sten escorts.

Fayid ablutions

So onto the road beside the Canal. Good surface except in patches. The sea stayed close to the road, looking rather like Heacham for many miles, dotted

Letters Home ~ 7

with little sailing boats. On one side the sea and sand flats, and on the other side bullrushes, beyond a salt collecting field, screened the Canal and anything beyond – (nothing tall enough to be visible).

A "copse" of Juniper (?) Trees first broke the monotony and we passed through an occasional native village. "Biblical" is hardly the word for the bucket and pole and bullock wheel water pumps feeding the fields here.

Out from this hint of civilisation we came to an area of real live sand dunes dotted occasionally with tufts of something grey-green, otherwise just sand. Here and there an army camp gave us an idea of what was waiting for us at the end of our ride.

Searchlights swept one old vehicle dump and made it like a film set for a prison camp epic – double barbed wire fences, the lot.

My other note gave an idea of the first hours here. A sand storm has raged most of the day but it died a bit this afternoon and we decided to explore the lido. A ten minute walk through a smelly village on a small canal (a donkey carcase complete with tail hung outside a butcher's) brought us to the Canal road, which we crossed, and there was the lake, water to the horizon, as big as the sea to all appearances. Ships on the Canal passage sailed palely in the distance.

From the beach runs a wooden planked pier which leads to where sand-filled barges have been sunk to fence off an area of swimming pool size.

We changed on the barges and after many hesitations dived into the cold green and rather doubtful water. That's when we found out why they're called the Bitter Lakes – Ugh! Strong salt with an undefinable something added.

At the Bitter Lakes lido.

Fayid, Sunday 27*th* March 1955

Yesterday, after my week on Fire Piquet, I reported for duty with my Shift and was put on an Auto Transmitter working to Malta – my first real live circuit.

I cleared eighteen messages, with the help of my partner on the Receive side, who showed me his job too. The main thing is to learn how to fill in the various Registers and time logs, and it is not a bit like Catterick. Anyway when we went on again for the night shift, four to ten your time, six to twelve here, my former partner was away on Guard so I stepped in to his more complicated job on Receive and another learner took over mine.

All went well and then as the traffic died away an old hand took over the pair of us and spent the evening chatting and really cluing us up on how it all really happens and what to forget of the things we learnt before.

Between the official messages the operator in Malta sent through such things as the Boat Race and National results, football scores, etc. it made an enjoyable change, and was to be a regular feature of Saturday night shifts.

Fayid Signal Centre.

Letters Home ~ 9

The Signal Centre here is a large Nissen hut with the Signal Office at one end with its various desks for clerks and the Officer in charge – DSO. The dividing wall is all window across his desk so that he can see into the "semi-auto" room where the three benches carry Transmit and Receive "autoheads" and teleprinters for the wireless links. Down one side are the Perforators which prepare the tapes and at the far end are the teleprinters connecting by land line to Port Said, Moascar, Suez, etc.

Fayid, Saturday 2nd April 1955

Temperature really going up, in the nineties now, one place near here was in the 105 region yesterday, and we are not far behind. Rather difficult picking out the NCOs on shift as everyone is stripped to the waist in the auto room during the day. The nights are officially cooler so we have to wear BDs after 6pm until the 21st of April. Sweating freely.

The other day I mounted two pages from my pocket sketch book for entry in the sketching section of the Exhibition here. Quite pleased with the result.

Fayid, April 12th 1955

Day trip to Cairo, yesterday, Easter Monday. I had booked an early call from the Guard, and got up at about 5 am, then joined the four others at their tent. We met the coach outside the YMCA bookshop at about 6 and started on our way around 6.15 am.

The sun was up before me and by this time it was broad day. Leaving Fayid, we passed the airport and followed the old road out into the desert. It's just a long straight macadamised track running direct from Fayid to the Sweet Water Canal at Ismailia.

Our two coaches were here joined by two others and we moved off in procession along the side of the canal, but not before my remark to a friend on the emerald green bird I had noticed on a hedge had caused such excitement that the bus nearly turned over. These lovely birds, about the size of a starling, became quite common along the road.

Ismalia bridge.

The land is more fertile near the water than at Fayid and the flat land is slashed with green and golden fields as it runs away into the distance. Some way back from the roadside, low, long farmhouses, striped pink and yellow along their length, stood knee high to the date palms around them.

We saw lots of workers in the fields, hoeing, and they would straighten up to watch us pass, then scratch themselves in a leisurely way before returning to their earth scratching labours.

The coach was upholstered in Rexine, and the seats were rather hard, so after about three hours of it we were happy to see an ever increasing number of houses by the road as we came into the edge of Cairo.

The main streets seem much like any other city, shops, neon signs, lots of traffic, etc. One thing which is noticed at a second glance is that the pavements are made of non-slip ridged tiles, of plain red, yellow, or black, arranged so that the whole pavement is striped in two foot bands of red or black and yellow from end to end.

The dust is thick and the colours are softened so that the effect is not immediately seen.

The second language for all posters etc. is French, and large numbers of French girls about the place aroused more interest among the troops in the party than anything else all day.

At last we drew up at the National Hotel and were invited to alight for a wash, and tea and cake. This came as breakfast for most of my particular group and we were ready for it by then, – about 9.30.

Soon after 10 we were off again to the Museum of Egyptian Antiquities, where the main treasures from the tomb of Tut-ankh-amen, other than those in the British Museum, are the prize exhibits. The Mummy cases of solid gold and gold leaf covered wood which fitted one inside the other about the Mummy itself, and much jewellery and a gold portrait head are all in a special barred room, closely guarded.

In the main gallery were endless rows of superb granite carvings or (as they were) rubbings, great rich forms over which play the rows of incised hieroglyphics. All of which are much like those in the Egyptian gallery of "the British" but somehow they seemed fresher and of course the light was brighter.

Up one staircase were framed papyrus scrolls, the strip cartoons of the Pharaohs, with fascinating doodly drawings on them. Alabaster vases I've only seen in books were here in all their wonder, including one specially cased and lit to show the decoration painted on an inner vase and only visible when lit from within.

I was thoroughly at home and could have stayed all day, but for the others – well perhaps the French girls were the only things they looked at with any interest. They were pleased therefore when the long-winded guide said he was sorry we hadn't time for the other galleries and led us back to the coach to drive to the Pyramids of Giza.

The road runs straight out from Cairo, and very soon it seemed we were right under the Great Pyramid of Cheops which rose apparently sheer up behind the roadside trees and from where I sat was far too high for the window to show me more than the base. As the coach swung round, the windows on my side faced it and I got the full view for the first time.

The Great Pyramid is not smooth but goes up to a fantastic height in steps of something like chest height. Tiny figures could be seen making their way to the top but we couldn't even contemplate the ascent with the time at our disposal.

When the guide at last stopped talking he led us round one side of the Pyramid to where two burial boats have recently been found, and passing this we came to where the land dipped suddenly, and found we were approaching the Sphinx from over his left shoulder as he lay in a hollow enclosed by a ruined courtyard beside the remains of a pink granite temple.

Egyptians swarmed about us offering rides on ponies, pony carts and camels, photos to be taken on any of them, and Pepsi-cola. The vivid bargaining and gesticulating crowd of them contrasted with the cool contemplative sphinx and the finality of the Great Pyramid on one side and the smaller pyramids behind.

Moving back to the Great Pyramid we were told that we had time to go inside. The entrance proper is now blocked but the vent shaft led up to the Queen's chamber about half way up inside.

Occasional electric lights showed us where to put our feet and what to fear for our heads as we walked the first level stretch from the exterior terraces. Then a wooden stair led up into the narrow shaft where a metal ridged cat-walk was fought for by streams of crouching laughing tourists passing sweating on their way up and down in the semi darkness. Those on the ascent excited and amused by the prospect of what might be ahead, – those now descending eager for the sunlight, and enjoying the malicious pleasure of seeing the new arrivals starting so eagerly on their strenuous clamber to the empty room which was all there was to see at the top.

Some eighteen or more feet high and about as long, the room is twelve feet wide and unfurnished except for a simple granite sarcophagus. It is entered by a 3½ ft opening at the bottom of one wall, and its only real point of interest was the perfection of its masonry, enormous granite blocks put together without mortar and with such perfect joints that the polished surface is hardly broken.

So down again, and into the coach to return to the hotel for lunch. This turned out to be very good: Savoury pie and salad followed by a good steak with chips and runner beans dressed with olive oil (the best way to serve them) and to finish, a jelly mould with banana slices and strawberries inset.

Lunch over we were off again to cram in some more sights and drove up to the Citadel. From here the city stretched away into the dusty haze which merged everything into a grey pool. The sun shone towards us across the city and made the dust more visible than the buildings. In the far distance we could see the two distinct groups of pyramids.

Within the Citadel stands the great Alabaster Mosque of Mohammed Ali and as the afternoon service came to an end we prepared to go inside. On our feet were tied canvas over-shoes and we padded into the open courtyard through which I had earlier seen a party of VIPs passing, bristling with red lapels and gold braid. One looked like Colonel Nasser to me but so many Egyptians look like that. Anyway, special guards stood about the Rolls at the gateway.

The inside was completely unfurnished and fitted with red patterned carpets. The countless chandeliers gave it an odd appearance of being a Victorian ballroom. The guide demonstrated the acoustics with a loud "ayeeee" which died slowly away in the vast dome. Above the first storey, panelled in polished alabaster, the walls, dome and semi-dome are richly painted with dummy columns and mouldings, friezes and patterns in the manner of the Islamic religious non-iconic decoration found in Santa Sophia, Constantinople.

From here we went to visit the Mousky Bazaars, I really don't know why, I suppose it's something to see, but the guide nearly lost us and nobody was at all wanting to go into the shops he led us to. Street vendors pushed bracelets, walking sticks – the lot – at us but no money could be spared even if we thought the prices right.

Safe in the coach again we were surrounded by a pack of vendors waving bananas, Pepsi-cola, sticks, sunglasses, rings and trinkets up to the windows, or begging cigarettes. I used the last two or three shots of the second film in my camera trying to get a couple of Arab children through the glass. Also tried drawing, them but in the hurly-burly it wasn't much good.

After tea at the hotel we had half an hour to ourselves before starting back to Fayid.

I bought stamps and then went for a walk with two friends. Again we met with determined vendors. A boot black who we refused was persistent and after three refusals tried an old trick here, loaded a brush with liquid polish and contrived to daub it across the toe cap of one of us without us knowing. He then appeared in front of us and offered to clean it off. His only reply from us was two sharp jabs in the ribs, so he left us.

We then started our three hour ride in the coach back to Fayid, where we were thoroughly ready for bed when we arrived towards 10 pm – a very full day.

Fayid, 23rd June 1955

...Numbers here dwindling with "demobs" and no replacements owing to impending move to Cyprus. Our CDSO has just sent a message to HQ Cyprus (our Main HQ), almost an SOS for more men, "Can struggle on with twelve more if you cannot send all I need."

Of course we all passed it round and read it before we sent it for him!

Getting Guards about every nine days now on top of the night shift every third night.

Fayid, 1st July 1955

...Well you certainly picked your moment to say you hoped I could let up now as the grind in the heat must be wearying.

On Wednesday I was off night shift, working until 4 am, and on the third day of a headache spell. I nearly went special sick at tea time as I was nearly delirious, with violent pains in the head and messages and perforated tapes racing before my eyes.

However Thursday was to be the great day of the Admin. Parade and Inspection and everyone was so busy I didn't want to bother the Orderly Sgt. with a special sick case. So I went on normal Sick Parade, Thursday morning – the only one there not getting off Admin. Parade, for which I had not been detailed.

The M.O. ordered me to bed for the day, -what a way to spend an Admin.! They gave me loads of Sulphaguanidine tablets as they thought I was due for a bout of dysentery, but that only resulted in constipation today so I'm off tablets. My head continued to swim all day. I felt exactly as I used to when we called it Migraine at home and I just took Codeine.

Anyway, this morning I had to report sick again and when I stood up first thing the headache descended like pushing my head through the ceiling. He has ordered me off all duties until I see him Monday.

Fayid, Sunday 3rd July 1955

...here's to tell you the complete rest over the weekend has brought me back to life as it were and I feel almost normal today, not full of bounce, but quite alive.

Now that it is all over, perhaps you'd be interested in the "flap" for the Admin. All tents here have a motley collection of home-made lockers in them for the three to six men in each tent. So, some weeks before Admin., a painting spree began, to get everything a standard dark green. The fever got hold of some people who proceeded to paint beds, brooms, buckets and tent poles as well. One or two painted their Windsor backed wooden chairs and then everything in sight. Guy ropes were tightened and tent walls rolled back at the sides – the sand around the tents is always swept into a neat striped pattern of ridges. After months of delay the new latrines were completed and the foul old ones at last destroyed – the one good event.

On the day before Admin., – when I had the headache really bad, – Wednesday, I helped in the marquee. All beds had gone and in their place was a selection of arm chairs and a couple of settees. Against the walls were tables carrying a range of newspapers, a large selection of magazines, educational supplements, and HM Stationery Office publications. There were odd low tables by the chairs for ash trays etc., and on one stood a portable gramophone with some records. This was our "rest tent" and most impressive and inviting it looked too, but like Cinderella's coach it disappeared at 12 on Thursday when the Admin. was safely over.

In the Signal Office, holes in the lino flooring were cut out and patched with fresh squares, and on night shift, when circuits were cleared, we painted all benches and windows. I was painting the Malta bench by myself at 3 am Wednesday morning. The Wednesday night shift used 14 lbs of car wax on a floor about 15 x 15 ft., and stayed up all night trying to get a shine on it for the first time in twelve months!

Fire buckets and signs were repainted and replaced, edgings whitewashed and stones cleared from areas and paths. The road into camp was swept and a swivel barrier put across it.

The corrugated iron surrounding the wash place was repainted but the crumbling concrete wash slabs stayed as they were.

Fayid – back of the NAAFI.

Fayid, Friday 15th July 1955 – 12 months done!

...I have been to the Education Centre and got a little plaster to start a small reclining figure. I'm giving it to John Morrison, who I met first in 3 Sqdn. 4TR, and who is earning it by posing in his swim trunks for me to draw, – hope it's a good one. Building direct on the wire with no files or proper tools is rather tricky, but fun, and it's the first for over twelve months so I'm not expecting too much.

John has a figure like my "Three boys", but his legs are very big seeming in some positions. He thinks the whole thing is a big joke and is quite good about posing, so far, when he's in the mood.

Fayid, 22nd July 1955

Had an extra day off today, so managed to finish the plaster figure, much to the amazement of all and sundry. Tools – one pen knife. John highly delighted. Taken photos.

Got a bit of good quality paper from the Education Centre on Wednesday so I hope to show some improvement in watercolours this weekend.

Fayid, 23rd July 1955 – Ismailia

I had the day off yesterday so I was fresh this morning and had a shower and generally messed about while the others recovered from their night shift.

Straight after dinner we caught an RAF Welfare bus and left Fayid by the famous Suez Canal Road. This skirts the Bitter Lake and then follows the Canal. The trip is worth making for the ride. The distance is about 35 Km in all.

We followed the edge of the lake for a long while, then suddenly I found I was looking at a long jetty-like spur which projects into the lake and was in fact the far side of the Canal. A moment later and we were running along beside the parallel straight or gently curving walls of the Canal. They slope at about sixty degrees for about six feet above the water and then the sand rises away in a gentle mound and lays away back in low hills to the distant horizon.

The road, in places, is just a few yards from the unprotected slope of the bank, while for much of the route, on its other side it is screened from the neighbouring land by a double row of conifers which give a welcome shade on the road.

Here and there the land rises by the Canal and the road detours through a wooded cutting to come out again above the Canal and then plunge down to rejoin the bank.

On one of these occasions we seemed to come right close to a superb new white-painted oil tanker "Olympic Wind".

By means of another jetty-like end to its walls the Canal gave at last into Lake Timsah and we once more skirted the lake and passed more varied and utilised areas, coming eventually to the outskirts of Ismailia, mud huts and a glimpse of the soaring booms, or whatever they are, of the dhow barges, above the trees by the Sweet Water Canal. Our bus crossed a little lifting bridge at a lock in the Canal before depositing us near the town centre, and we saw many of these low, broad vessels with their dead flat ends and almost water-level sides.

We wandered first around the streets and window-shopped, but nothing tempted. Then we walked on the grass by the Sweet Water just for the pleasure of walking on grass, and looked across at the "out of bounds" park on the other side. Then we went in search of further lemonade and met a Carnival in the streets.

Egypt was, of course in "Fiesta" today, as it is the third anniversary of the end of Farouk. The floats were rather drab and all rather similar – the flowers and creepers on some were really funny, they were so wilted! One float represented Coca-Cola, the national drink of Egypt as we call it. The best thing in the show was a policeman on a restive horse, lovely to watch as it side stepped up the road, tense and crisp in its movements. Even the watching crowd lost some of its sheep-like stupor when the horse appeared.

I couldn't help comparing the Carnival here and its odd air of self consciousness and drab "corn" with the verve and contagious atmosphere of "Fiesta" in Fornalutx.

Hunger then drove us into Costas restaurant for egg and chips. We ate our food in a roofless courtyard shaded in part by a trellis from which grew cucumbers. Cats and a monkey added to the distractions, and the place was thick with enormous potted palms etc. I shocked my party by putting olive oil as well as vinegar on the salad. One thought it was a hair dressing.

Fayid – sleeping Signalman Topliss.

The other two wanted to go to a film so John and I made our way to the 6.30 pm bus back to Fayid. As we left "Ish" the sun was setting low in the sky and with the glare of full day removed I was occupied the whole trip by the extraordinary way in which everything acquired new colour.

The dusty pallor of the journey out was gone and the sand dunes ahead added a sort of phosphorescent glow to the last light from the sky behind us. Ploughed strips of land had become deep purple brown in the new light, contrasting richly with the intense new emerald colour of the American corn patches, and a boat drawn up on the beach had exchanged its dusty brown for a deep red which glowed against the now deep turquoise lake stretching away to the mauvey horizon, where a few lights had begun to sparkle.

Before the light had really begun to go, we passed, some distance from "Ish", a strange little building, purpose unknown, striped dark brick-red and yellow, with a mid-green door and a pale blue dome on top, rather face-like, with its orange slatted windows, standing alone on a little hillock with only a few mud and straw huts within hailing distance – odd.

So back to Fayid, where we were in need of yet another fizzy before going back to camp. Not such an exciting outing as the Cairo trip but it does make a change of scenery and I have had a good look at the great Canal now.

Bedspace at Fayid.

Fayid, Friday 29th July 1955

...Today, off night shift, I got up on top of the tent, and with sun glasses and hat to protect from glare, drew in ink the camp from there, tent lines with parade ground in middle distance and lake visible on horizon. Then took off dark glasses and, though precariously perched, managed to splash watercolours in more or less the right places.

... Paper is a wonderful treat. Arms and legs got rather scorched by the sun in the one or one and a half hours taken, and being rather conspicuous up there I have added to the number of people in camp convinced I'm mad!

Fayid, 20th August 1955

... Had an interesting day yesterday and an interesting morning today.

Today we were on Fatigues, as is usual when it is our day for afternoon shift.

They packed the lot of us into a truck and took us about ten miles to the transmitters aerial field to lower or "drop" an aerial mast, – an eighty or ninety foot effort of tubular steel.

There is an enormous area of flat pebbly sand from which rise the slender masts and their web of stay wires. The masts are painted black and white, like Belisha beacons, and stand rather oddly in the enormous plain. Behind runs the great ridge of sand hills, jagged ridges and strata standing boldly out from the sweeping slopes of windswept yellow sand. The whole backdrop shimmering when seen through the deep layer of heat waves which ruffle the air across the aerial field.

We had to attach a mast section to the foot of the mast as a derrick, transfer one set of stay wires to it, and then lower the mast gently by resisting its weight by a set of pulleys attached to the derrick. When the mast was down, the derrick was vertical in its place, and that was then lowered to one side.

Yesterday I got up for 8 am breakfast after a good night shift and packed my little box with brushes, pencil, paints, rag, ink, and paint water bottle. Then I walked along the railway line to the open air swimming pool at "Olympia", the sports centre, and went on the sun roof I've discovered on the Naafi. From there earlier in the week I had painted the pool, and yesterday I faced the other way, due South, and found the flat land running away along beside the lake was worth trying.

The "best polo ground in the Canal Zone" in the foreground is succeeded by a rugby pitch edged with a row of little dark trees which serve to throw back the receding ploughed fields, corn crops and waste ground which run into the distance, where a line of camps gives a dark edge to the foot of the dominating sand cliffs, which turned purple as their furthest ridges caught the shadow of slight cloud.

Fayid Education Centre.

By this time I was somewhat scorched by the sun, so, after taking some snaps of shadows cast by a pergola below me, I went for a swim in the pool and bought cakes for lunch. Later I walked through the native village and along to the barge lido where I sat in the shade of some trees and tried another painting, this time of the WVS lounge and games room facing the lake. Bit of a mess.

My drawing board is a success. When I got all that stuff from the Education Centre just before it closed, I grabbed two pieces of cardboard to support my bundle. Now I hold them together with elastic garters which also serve to hold the ends of my sheets of paper. When I start out I have three or four sheets of paper between the boards, and when I want to draw I pull a sheet out and slip its ends under the elastic and carry on. The completed drawing is slipped back between the two cards.

Weight – less than my large sketch books.

Fayid, 5th September 1955

We are down to very short staff again, with me as 2 i/c and doing Superintendent next Sunday morning.

We went on our trip to Bir Odebe on the Gulf of Suez at the top of the Red Sea, and what a time we had! Just to get away from this camp was a treat in itself.

Uniform was the dress, as it is outside the Zone, and we also took four rifles and two Stens, but apart from that we were hardly military at all. The M.T. Troop laid on two lorries, a ration truck and a trooper, and thirty of us, including Mr. Blair, my Troop Officer, piled in with stacks of food, blankets, lemonade, ice etc., and me with my paints and paper – optimist.

Left camp on Saturday about 3 pm, then a rough ride of about three hours along the bumpy tarmac known as the Treaty Road towards Suez. The landscape is so similar all along, a flat plain running to the foot of the sand cliffs and slopes, that the truck seemed to be getting nowhere. It was a pity we could not use the Canal Road.

However, at last we saw in the distance the oil storage tanks of Suez and beyond, the sea, dotted with white ships.

Skirting Suez we pressed on to the right and left the sight of the sea and cut across the middle of another barren, arid plain. The hills were well back in the distance all along to our right. Then suddenly they cut out towards the sea and within a few miles had come close and almost forced the road into the sea edge which advanced on us from the other side. For several hundred yards the road scrambled along the foot of the cliffs, its seaward edge broken and sheer to the sea about twelve feet below, crystal clear and calm.

Soon the land opened into a bay and the road again took up its position between the sea and the cliffs, well away from either. We passed a number of similar "trips" parked by the beach and then turned off the road and stopped out of sight of anyone else on a stretch of the beach where the road was furthest from the sea.

The trucks parked alongside one another and out we all got to settle in. No tent had been brought, so that saved a lot of bother. We had parked right by some old box wood and a former camp's fire site so we soon had a good fire and tea in the making.

Darkness was on us before long but the full moon was bright enough for anything -so we didn't regret forgetting to bring lamps. Sausage, fried bread and tomatoes, bread and jam and tea – more than I could eat. Then we settled into our little groups and made our little camps all about the beach over about 100 yards of sand.

Letters Home ~ 23

We had all been for a swim while waiting for the tea, before the light failed, but most of us went in again by moonlight. All being tired we then settled ourselves for the night, digging holes for hips etc., and folding blankets as sleeping bags. Some people are crazy though.

I proceeded to paint the wagon and the setting by the light of the moon as I sat on my kit.

I could see the tone fairly well but had to hope that I really was only dipping in the black and blue pans!

Trucks by moonlight at Bir Odebe.

Then, with a couple of bottles of fizz as standby, I too snuggled down very comfortably under the stars about twenty yards from the water's edge.

We had to take turns to wander about "on guard", so I was woken at about 3.30 am for a very pleasant 30 mins. stroll in the moonlight. All the rest huddled in their blankets and only the sound of the sea. Then handing over the watch I snuggled down and dropped off again. When I awoke about 5.30 or 6 someone had the fire going under the tea water and with the sun a few degrees over the horizon and not yet hot I got a mug of tea and sat in "bed" painting the view north along the beach.

Then there was time for a swim before a breakfast of cornflakes and tinned milk with a dash of water, and pineapple. Then bacon, potatoes, (tinned but good) beans and fried egg – bread and jam.

We lazed and swam and drank lemonade and tea, until the DSO, who had mucked in very well, said he wanted to take one truck back along the beach to where there was a coral reef. So those who wanted to go too piled in and off we went while another party attempted to climb the cliff.

The coral was about twenty to thirty yards out in six feet of water and when we stood on it we were able to keep our heads above water. My goggles paid for themselves yet again on this occasion. The coral was

24 ~ *Letters Home*

pale pinky mauve spikey stuff and smooth blue formations, and from it sprouted apple green fluffy weed. The fish were really wonderful and being quite crazy I went ashore and came back armed with some old cigarette packets and a soft pencil with which I made five drawings as the selected fish came back in sight. Then I got back in the truck and made colour roughs from the pencil notes.

One fish was shaped like a female Swordtail, about four inches long, with royal blue head and stripes and black tail and stripes interlocking with the blue. Another was like the Spades on playing cards, brick red at its head and black at its tail with grey in the middle and white stripes V shaped from top to bottom, about six inches long – the grey middle darkening towards the tail.

Back to "camp" for lunch of stew – everything had been thrown in but it wasn't bad (or we were very hungry). Then last swims and we began to pack up. Tins and an unused box of kippers safely buried, and all bottles collected (for money back) we piled in and started off.

Disaster could not wait any longer and the radiator blew up just short of Suez. The driver poured in water and set off again but he soon pulled up to report to the DSO, who was now driving the 3 tonner, that his fan belt had packed up and his engine was red hot. So we parked while the DSO went into Suez for a new belt – time for a quick drawing of Suez oil tanks and refineries!

But when they got back the belt would not fit so we cruised for a few miles to a filling station where we tried to borrow a rope for towing. An army truck pulled up and lent us a cable and hook and we progressed very slowly. All very thirsty.

Then the cable snapped and we stuck. Another truck offered a lift so we split into three parties. Some piled into the DSO's truck, some went in the lift, and six and the driver stayed to guard the truck. We really sped now. I was in the truck with the DSO and he put his foot down hard and we sped through the dark – it was quite dark by then. At the first British camp he pulled in and phoned for a relief truck to be sent for the other one, collecting him where he was, while the rest of us were run back to a late tea at about 7.30 – 8, tired, dry, and sunburned.

The "rescue" was quick and the DSO came in to see that we'd all been fed – wonderful bloke – he looked quite worn out and was thick grease to the elbow.

So it all ended safely and apart from a touch of sunburn on my neck I'm no worse for a hectic weekend. Total cost – 10 piastres or two shillings.

Fayid – view from the Naafi.

5th November 1955 Episkopi – 3 GHQ move from Fayid, Egypt, to Episkopi, Cyprus

I was on extra night shift Thursday, after the afternoon shift. Went up at ten and helped in odd jobs, although I felt I wasn't really needed. Only two of my own shift stayed, the others were sent back.

The excitement of the DSO and CDSO on finally closing "London" – last London/Egypt direct link and all that, was quite amusing. We had to clear all outstanding traffic on hand and then the DSOs at each end had a little chat and we pulled the plugs out.

Immediately mechs set to work and the whole place was stripped of equipment as each bench became free. All paper had to be burnt etc.

With lots of people just standing about yawning, at about 2.30 am several people decided it was time for bed and slipped off, and feeling quite worn out and doing nothing at the time I followed and got to bed about 3 am. I got away with a telling off from Mr. Blair, but should have been charged for absence from duty!

Bed 'till about 5.15 , then a wash and hand-in bedding. Then breakfast (poor), and hand-in plates, then clear scraps from tents and wait.

At 8 am assemble at gate with all kit, cross road to Office, where all kit was weighed. 66lbs allowed and mine weighed 66lbs! Then a 200 yd. walk to board trucks which then drove to where we had just weighed the kit! So, to the airport and the RAF had to weigh the kit again. We had just changed £1 and 10/- notes to Cyprus money and had odd Egyptian change to use up. Cyprus money is very attractive. The new decimal currency is just out so it's nearly all brand new and nice to handle. More waiting, then to a lecture room for instructions on behaviour on plane, use of life saver and a few scraps of info on the trip. Then we walked across to the "Valetta".

I was near the front when we got to the ladder, by hook or by crook, and boarded among the first. Chris Cooper had got me a front seat right by the pilot's cabin, in front of the wing. Rear seats were reserved for Officers, behind wing , so most of the others saw only wing. Door shut and locked, and a word from the Pilot. Trip about 1 3/4 hrs., height about 7500ft., ground speed about 150 mph and so on.

Take off, after the procedure of revving and taxiing about, was smooth, and the climb that followed very rapid, the sand dropped and sank in detail beneath us and we banked across for a last glimpse of the fertile area about the "sweet water".

The Suez Canal was on the wrong side and I couldn't see it. (The other front window was blocked with baggage). But I glimpsed Lake Timsah and then we were over bald stretches of sand dunes heading for the dark green-brown coast strip.

For many miles before the actual sea line the land is a mass of sand and mud banks, marshes and patches of weed or slime and great pools and lakes. The land masses making weird patterns of fantastic shapes, intertwining curves and knife edge ridges. Dhow sails, triangular specks of white on the blue-black green-black water, and on the most unlikely sites, the rings of mud walled enclosures marked the mud banks as inhabited.

At last a final bank, of smoother and more simple outline, edged with gentle surf, showed us where Africa ended and the Mediterranean began. Below us now appeared the line of ships making for and from the entrance to the Canal and after this nothing but the smoothness of the sea.

We dozed, in spite of the engines' roar, until one of the crew left his seat by the Pilot to hand out slices of fruit cake and paper cups of orangeade.

I could, by turning in my seat, watch the crew of four in their bucket seats which slide on tracks in the cockpit floor. The Wireless Op. had the same type of receiver as my ex-RAF one, and a transmitter to match. He tapped Morse and scribbled notes for the Pilot and Navigator throughout the trip.

If I stood up I could look out at the front, and I bobbed up at intervals to catch the first glimpse of the island ahead. At last, through thin cloud, I could make out a thin yellow line of coast beach which showed bright in the sun shining from behind us. As we approached we saw clearly the curious axe-blade peninsular of Akrotiri which juts southwards between the bays of Limassol and Episkopi. We crossed the coast by Limassol and turned east along the coastal plain, safety belts fastened to keep us seated as we met the bumps in the air over the hilly land.

The island rises smoothly in gentle humps of whitish yellow, speckled with shrubs and trees right to the tops. Later, we came to the plain approaching Nicosia. There the uplands were a sandy red colour, flat and crisp edged, and from these edges the land fell away sharply into the "lowland" not far below. The sandy red patches were interspersed with dusty grey-green and yellow in the fields and farms.

Oranges in certain spots, elsewhere olives, olives, olives, unmistakable with their silver grey foliage. Unlike Mallorca the olives here grew all over the place, not in steep walled terraces.

The ground came up nearer as we turned gently in to the landing strip and in a moment we were taxiing round the tarmac to the aircraft park by the Customs Office. Silence, as the engines stopped, deafness, popping in the ears and a sense of unreality as we waited for the Pilot to put on his KD jacket again and be ready to open the door.

Quickly across the tarmac to the Office, where they checked on Vaccination Certs., and asked anything to declare, wirelesses, watches, cigs. etc. – they seized a packet of cigarette papers as forbidden goods! – then through a passage to a Naafi for a delicious tomato roll and tea. Out again to a ramshackle motor coach and we set off for the drive of about 2 ½ hours to Episkopi followed by a truck with our kit.

Through the outskirts of Nicosia we were led by a Despatch Rider carrying a Sten across his lap. The streets, often narrow, were completely free of any sign of military goings on. Slogans in Greek plastered most of the whitewashed walls. We drove through the late sunshine, and I was amazed at the buildings being constructed everywhere, houses, shops, everything. Many very contemporary and adventurous designs, colourful and clean, balconied flats and houses with verandahs. The ironwork over the doors and the effect generally gave me many reminders of Mallorca even before we reached the countryside and its olives.

The town passed, we changed our D.R. for a guard with a rifle, who stood in the cab of the baggage lorry behind our coach. On we raced towards the hills, the driver keeping up an amazing speed along a road tarred in the middle with cobbled side strips for use only in passing other vehicles. Up hills and down, skirting valleys and doubling back on ourselves on the other side of a gully. Up and round, down and across. Everywhere the roads are newly improved and bridges replaced by new, neater, wider ones with white handrails, the old bridges standing parallel to one side, barricaded and often demolished.

The sun was now quite low and its angled rays picked up the hills and clouds and gave added richness to the colours. At one place several fairytale mounds of silver sand, thick speckled with rich dark green, stood out clearly from the deep blue of the distant ranges, and above all, from a mass of deep blue cloud, reared a great rugged mass of white cloud, tinged gold in the brilliant light which threw crisp shadows across its forms.

This cloud remained alight when the sun had sunk from our view into the layer of blue cloud above the horizon. And later, when it was dark, I saw that this same cloud mass had spread and fanned up and over like a great cockle shell, cupped towards us, and in its hollow form, sudden flashes of sheet lightning threw into relief first one and then another of its components.

The darkness outside and the lights inside the coach had by now turned the windows into mirrors, and even in the streets of Limassol, as we rushed through, it was hard to see much until, ahead and to the left we glimpsed the lights of Episkopi.

The first hutments looked promising as we stopped by them, but the Sgt. who stood to meet us called out "Officers' Mess". However the two DSOs, Messrs Hopkins and Blair, wanted to see us all safely fixed and they stayed on as we drove higher to pass great silver Nissen huts and we came to a halt by the power station.

Unloaded, we dumped our kit on the roadside and with eating irons at the ready made for the cookhouse, where we were promised the first meal since breakfast at 6 am. Horror! The hot plate had on it a few trays of lumpy Pom, cold fatty meat and some sort of pudding. However, after a little fuss and a wait of 25 minutes we got fried eggs (twice as big as Egyptian ones) a tinned sausage, and chips, with good tea and stewed apricots.

Then to collect bedding and get tents. Mr. Blair was still about as we got back to our kit, loaded with mattress, four blankets, two sheets, a pillowcase and a bedside mat. All, except the pillow, brand new, and the blankets smell wonderful.

We have two L/Cpls on our shift, so they got a tent each, and Mr. Blair told Taff Griffiths and myself (we were on the tin-wash at 4TR together) to be i/c the other two tents and asked us to choose who we wanted to be with us.

Our tents have no current on 'till Monday so we had a hurricane lamp. First in, and i/c, I chose the single bed on the right as I went in. The other single bed was soon bagged, leaving the two double bunks for the taking.

There is a good light fitting and a big white plastic shade, a socket for an iron, and the floor, of smoothish concrete slabs, is crossed by three strips of coconut matting, 18 yds in all. The remaining floor can be covered by our bedside mats if we want to be lush.

As yet we have no lockers, or any hope of lockers, but we may get a tin box on Monday.

So, after Naafi break, to bed. My mattress is so new it's lumpy-bumpy, but I don't remember worrying. A Sgt. woke me this morning, but he wanted someone else so I dozed off again and we missed breakfast in my tent.

Mr. Blair called in just as I was back from a wash, and told us we have today off.

The camp: The daylight explained a lot of things which were most confusing in the dark, and we can see something of the place. We perch in terraces on the side of a hill crowned by the power house. The vibrations from the power house carry through the ground to our tents and the beds, and a constant noise like an engine turning over, and a throbbing sensation in the head, is something we'll all have to get used to. Steep concrete paths snake down the slope through gorse bushes and shrubs. Below the next row of tents in front of mine as we face across the valley, are Nissen huts for showers, lavs and wash houses, and past these the hill drops away to the bottom where the large Naafi nestles in a space cleared of the prickles.

Up the other side gorse again fights for survival between huge areas of building activity and great buildings and roads are under construction all over the hill.

The hill top is distinguished by a low red roofed cluster, our Signal Centre, and near-by are the aerials for the Navy.

Just heard there was hot water in the shower house, so dashed there for a treat – first hot wash since last March! Bunch of grapes for "afters" at dinner today.

Episkopi, 15th November 1955

…Went for a long walk, first since I got here. Walked across valley to Sig. Cen. and then left to cliff top. It's a terrific drop to a sort of coast plain with shrubs, a beach strip and then the sea. There is an enormous bay with headlands either side. I went along cliff to left, across headland to smaller bay, then turned up a gulley and so round back to camp.

On cliff top I had to pick my way between shrubs, gorse, pine and various conifer seedlings or small trees, all rather stunted. The whole area is a sort of patchwork of earth and plants with great slabs of smooth greyish rock rising slightly proud of the earth. Pine needles cushion the feet, and the general greenness is spotted with little flowers, some like little buttercups, some frail white crocus-like ones. And all over the place great thick sproutings like tulips or hyacinths coming up. The arrival of the wet season has probably stimulated all sorts of late growth and the pine shrubs are bright green with new needles.

I disturbed a great many "hoppers" of various sizes and lizards from 1 ½ to about 9 inches long scuttled across the rocks as I walked.

The cliff face itself is a pale golden colour, dazzling bright in the sun,- the line of cliffs I had seen from the 'plane as we came in. It is quite strongly marked in strata horizontally and is fluted vertically in a bold right-angled section. As I progressed along the cliff to the left I could see, beyond the next headland, the great flat peninsular, which from where I stood lay completely below the horizon. The sun, shining more or less straight at me from that direction, made the strip of land a dark shape across a blaze of reflected light.

Elsewhere the water is a most intense blue. They say it's too cold for a swim now but I think some time this week I'll clamber down that far for a dip.

At last we each have a locker in the tent and they've also issued each tent with a 6 ft trestle table so we have a degree of comfort.

Episkopi, 23rd November 1955

(Please excuse writing as hands very cold)

... Night before last it rained heavily during the night and at 3 am I was fixing tent flap and evacuating my stuff to middle of tent. 6-ish we all got up, and it started to rain again. In a moment a terrific squall hit the camp. Thunder, lightning, half inch hail stones, and gale. The tent walls lifted and we clung on to them and dragged kit to the middle, laughing our heads off as it all seemed so crazy, half dressed, cold, wet, and not sure if the lot would sail away! The roof of the lavs did sail. Ten yards of corrugated iron roof with timber supports, it lifted up the hill, over the first line of tents a good thirty paces up the slope, across the ten paces between the rows, to hit the tent next but one to mine, flatten it, and pile up behind it, for all the world like a 'plane crash.

Fortunately the only injury was one bloke in the tent, who needed two stitches in his forehead.

No "first works" that day. We went to breakfast in ground sheets and waited there for trucks, which came late, to take us on shift. We spent the afternoon putting stakes, rocks and earth on the tent walls to hold them in future. Wet and cold now.

...Last Sunday afternoon about five of us joined the many who made their way down the goat track to the bottom of the cliff and thence through the bushes and shrubs for three or four hundred yards to the sea.

The Med. was cold at first, but once in, great fun. The breakers were so different from the Bitter Lake and Red Sea on the other occasions when we've bathed. The level dropped away suddenly a few yards out so we spent our time in the shallows. The pebbles seem more patterned than I've seen before, with stripes and patches of many colours. There's just a strip of pebbles at the water line with sand inland and under water, then some thirty paces inland a ridge of "bunkers" with shrubs, and so down to the flat plain right to the foot of the cliffs. The track mounts steeply along the cliff face, hairpin doubling all the way, a sort of gulley with a 2 – 3 ft wall of rock and shrubs on the outside in parts, the path worn into rough steps in places.

... Had a horrible night shift last night, they are all much the same, and 6 pm 'till 8 am is a long time.

The signal is often bad owing to the weather and you spend all night trying to clear traffic or making copies (printing tapes on the teleprinter in the office) for sending by DR or 'plane if wireless means fail.

Then, under the present system, the five or six hundred tapes of the day must be packed in large labelled envelopes and stacked; all rooms swept, etc, and preparations made for the day, before morning shift arrives. If we got two whole days off afterwards I'd say we earned them. We get to bed about 9 am, sleep 'till 3 pm (missing dinner), get up for tea, write letters, then early bed, feeling dizzy. I should start looking my age (at least) shortly!

Episkopi, 24th November 1955

...The RSM detailed five of us to put a new top on his tent.

We found afterwards there's an easy way to do this, but a crazier hour of tent erection would be hard to find.

Tents here are lashed to a frame of posts, and we first had to untie all the stay ropes on the outer roof. Then two of us got up between the roofs and pushed the "outer" up off the pins in the top of the poles. Sitting astride the end of the inner roof we then had to ease the whole outer roof over to one side to emerge in daylight at last. The new roof was tied to the ropes of the old, and as the three at the bottom pushed and pulled the new and old respectively, the two of us at the top eased it over the ridge pole and then over our heads like a shirt until we could get the little reinforced holes over the pins. This done we escaped from the folds and set about lashing the ropes to the wood frame and pulling the roof tight. Sounds simple enough but they are quite a size and this one was double thickness and damp so it weighed quite a bit.

Episkopi, 29th November 1955

... We're back on three-shift working after the trial of four-shifts, with Guards and Fire Picquets on days off so there's not much time for anything except sleep.

I was on night shift Saturday, walked back at 7.30 am Sunday in time for Mass as usual, then managed to get something for breakfast and went to bed.

A friend got me two meat pies from the Naafi at ten and I went to sleep then until 4 pm. Had to be on Guard at 4.30. Everything ready except shave fortunately, so I just made it. We had gone onto State of Emergency – Active Service on Saturday night so everyone was rather nervous as we expected trouble.

Not much sleep during "off" periods so I felt pretty grim in the morning.

Breakfast, and bed. Was wakened at eleven, and I cleaned up for dinner at twelve. Then shift from one to six. By the end of a hectic afternoon I was past sleep so I popped off to the first night of the gramophone records at the Edn. Centre. LP performance of Carmen. By the end of Act II it was about 8.30 pm, so I came back to bed. Slept 'till 6 am today. Shift this morning, bags of traffic from yesterday to be cleared still. I can't find the tapes so tonight will be hectic.

... "Muggins" now runs the ZDK dept. with the assistance of two newcomers who have to be shown what to do. (ZDK = re running uncleared messages)

Red Sea Fish.

Fayid Camp, Egypt ~ back of shops as seen from camp.

Fayid Camp, Egypt ~ barbed wire perimeter fence.

Fayid Camp, Egypt ~ the view from my tent roof (see page 20).

Fayid Camp, Egypt ~ interior of tent.

Fayid Camp, Egypt ~ tent interior.

Fayid Camp, Egypt ~ the Naafi pool.

Egypt ~ Bitter Lake Lido.

Fayid Camp, Egypt ~ outlook from the Author's tent.

Fayid Camp, Egypt ~ camp petrol station and evening sky.

Fayid Camp, Egypt ~ petrol station viewed from camp.

Fayid Camp, Egypt ~ Reception tent.

Fayid Camp, Egypt ~ Squadron Office.

Fayid Camp, Egypt ~ view through tents.

Cyprus ~ Episkopi Bay.

Cyprus ~ Episkopi Bay ~ dead calm.

Cyprus ~ Episkopi Bay ~ looking east.

Cyprus ~ Episkopi ~ Christmas in the tent.

Cyprus ~ Episkopi ~ tents and view.

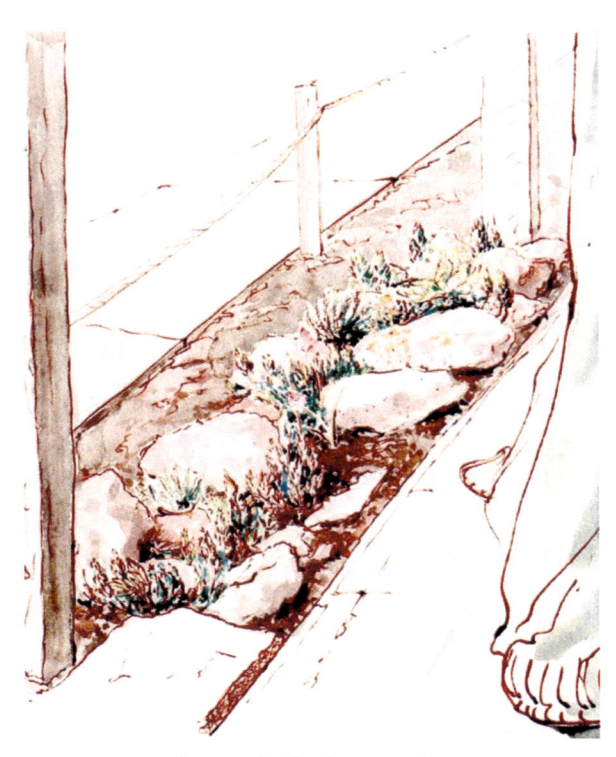

Cyprus ~ Episkopi ~ tent garden.

Cyprus ~ Episkopi ~ tent rock garden.

Cyprus ~ Episkopi ~ tents ~ June 1956.

Cyprus ~ Episkopi ~ the view from my bedspace.

Cyprus ~ Happy Valley ~ carob tree.

Jerusalem ~ Garden of Gethsemane ~ olive tree.

Cyprus ~ Episkopi ~ building work in progress.

Cyprus ~ Episkopi ~ morning after EOKA bomb attack (see pages 75/6).

There's enough work for six experienced people on the ZDK desk so it's not really surprising that we can't always clear up the mess left by previous shift.

Episkopi, 13th December 1955

The "chos" is almost completely over here for the present, and my job is a lot easier. Also my assistants are quite well trained now. DSO, Miss Sharland was very pleased last Sunday night shift as we cleared and closed Malta all clear both ways on both circuits, ie nothing owing either way right up to date for the first time since Episkopi opened. Then did the same on all circuits to make the first perfect hand-over to the morning shift – "chuffed".

Episkopi, Christmas 1955

... Herewith some account of my first Christmas abroad written in instalments as and when possible over the weekend.

Friday night I had a busy time on shift but closed near enough all clear to date and having made out Traffic States for the next shift came back about six instead of waiting until eight. Dawn, breaking as we walked across the valley revealed the camp festooned with toilet rolls and all the signs of a hectic night – not one fire bucket left standing etc and a plate trolley from the dining hall some 300 yards off in the camp. Sunday routine was the order for Christmas Eve, so, with breakfast not 'till 7.15 I had a hot bath before anyone else got up.

Breakfast – a sausage and two slices of bread and marmalade – then bed, but not to sleep for long as those not just off night shift made quite a racket in the tent. Under my bed was a bottle of Commanderia, a Cyprus wine at 5/- a bottle which a friend had bought for me. That is not to be touched until tomorrow. The others in the tent have supplies of cheap local brandy and whisky – rather like meths by the smell . We all passed out nibbles of various biscuits, dates and sweets and dozed between times. Then I started roughing out a drawing of the tent with decorations , to finish later, and we got up for dinner – haddock, peas and spuds, and an orange. Not much of a meal, and no tea or coffee with it.

I'm off all Christmas Day, on night shift if needed Boxing Day and off all the next day, so it's quite a break – no Guards or Fire Picquets either!

There are drunkards lolloping and shouting round the camp all day today and I suppose there will be for the whole weekend. Every tent holds its stocks of illicit booze – hope nobody has a surprise inspection.

Two of "the tent" got a H.P. Radio from the Squadron Office while I was on shift last night – it may be OK but so far only one station is free from terrific atmospherics, this place, as I told you, is thick with electrical storms.

I climbed on the roof today to add an aerial but there's little effect from that or the earth.

Sky overcast this morning, but earlier in the week it has been lovely warm sunny weather and I've noticed wild spring flowers coming out.

On Guard Wednesday night I enjoyed the spectacle of the dawn over Akrotiri peninsular – dark on the sea – quite something about 5.45 am, the salt lake gleaming dully in the dark land mass.

Have I told you how I decorated the tent? with silver paper flowers dotted all over the inside of the roof and a little red crepe paper in sort of garters at intervals up the poles over a crisscross of pink paper tape. All lockers sporting a display of Christmas cards – I didn't do very well, only got four.

Tea, Christmas Eve, 1955

I went soon after 4 pm, as it's Sunday routine, but tea started about 4.30. The doorway was crammed with drunks; a fight nearly started but one of the contestants was so far gone he passed out. The Cook Cpl. yelled in vain for order and said even if it was Christmas this was a Dining Hall and not a football match. He was quite far gone too, as were all the kitchen staff. But the stew served was good, and the rice to follow. The meal was absolute Bedlam, with snatches of bawdy songs and Carols, cat calls and the crash of lurching bodies against the tubular steel chairs. I almost wished I was to be on shift tonight.

From the window, as I had waited, I had watched Santa Claus arrive at the Sgts. Mess children's party, seated on the bonnet of a car, his sack of toys in the boot. We don't normally see any kids as the married quarters are in Limassol. Quite a crowd, and they all looked nice in their party frocks and bright pullovers. Proud fathers clutched the verandah posts for support as they watched.

I got back from tea just as the rain started. Non-stop pour-down ever since.

The first drunk called about eight, shook hands all round, called me a grand old sweat, then left in disgust as we had no beer for him. The main crowd is off to the cookhouse for Tombola and beer so I may get a chance to play with the radio.

Tombola off, so they're all back.

10 pm, Bawdy beer party with brandy lacings going on in the tent. Pouring with rain outside. Not the ideal preparation for Midnight Mass I'm afraid and not eating or drinking makes it rather awkward when my presence is remembered. I've been sitting in the corner trying to paint the scene – horrible mess of wet paint and smudged ink. Broke my nib in the process and the light makes the colour of doubtful value. I wanted a record of the effect of bottles on the table and the decorations originally but that's not what I got. About 28 bottles on the table – beer, brandy and wine – for six. They will be in quite a state by the time I get back from church at this rate.

(Note : In 1986 this painting, with one of Fayid, was borrowed by the Imperial War Museum for their National Service Exhibition)

Sounds of smashing bottles along the path. Other parties in other tents will not be getting the money back on their bottles.

Bedlam.

One parcel contained Crackers, so we are all wearing paper hats.

Midnight Mass, Christmas 1955

The party decided to move next door about 11.20 so I tidied up the tent, dumped all bottles in the rubbish box and added to my little hoard of sweets, biscuits, and a tumbler of wine in my locker. Then I tidied myself and went off to Mass. The rain had stopped by then and I joined a little crowd waiting by the church tent for someone to come and find the light switch. Someone did, and we went in.

The marquee had been furnished with concrete floor covered with matting, tubular chairs and wooden kneelers. The Altar is a large, rather elegant table on which stands a small Tabernacle with Cross. The altar cloths had been rescued earlier from the puddles and were replaced for Mass. The end roof of the tent is a rich dark brown, the end wall lined with white, and the wall/roof joint decorated with wisps of fir tree, a bunch of sprigs also being tied to each tent pole just above head level. Each side of the Altar stood a large potted red poinsettia.

As the church filled, an occasional disturbance was caused by odd drunks dashing for the door to be sick. I was somewhat shaken to see so many of my own friends and acquaintances of the Signals present, lapsed Catholics making their annual compromise – I had no idea so many of them were supposed to be Catholic.

I arrived back to find the tent in darkness. Two of the three had got into bed, the third lay on his, unable to remove his boots until I came back to help.

The tent was more or less as tidy as I had left it and having sluiced down the sick from the doorway with a bowl of water, I had my biscuits and glass of wine and got to bed – though not before two marauding drunks had come in, one looking for his friend, the other looking for a striped table sunshade taken from the Naafi as he wanted to decorate something with it.

I must have gone straight off as I next found it was morning and the Sgts, cold and damp in their overcoats and a mixture of clothes were coming round with a bucket of coffee and rum. I got up and opened the tent flap for them and got out all the mugs for the others – now awake, but I was the only one able to drink and enjoy the sickly brew!

Breakfast was good. Tinned tomatoes, a sausage, an egg and bacon, with corn flakes and good tea, bread and marmalade. It poured with rain as I ate but had pretty well stopped by the time I came back. Numerous raging drunks making fools of themselves at breakfast. Back in the tent we heard part of the service of nine carols from Cambridge on the General Overseas Service.

Dinner is to be at 1 pm, served by the WOs and Officers. Hope it will not rain then. In uniform, of course.

Still rainy and rainbowy at 10.30 am, rather cold too.

Christmas Dinner was fine. We got there about 12.30 to find a largish queue already, most of them pretty high and switching from near bawdy songs to carols and the well known "Why are we waiting?" to the tune of "Come all ye faithful. The suspense built up nicely and at last we were let in.

The small square tables were arranged in two solid lines the length of the hall and were dressed with cloths, crackers, cigs, sweets, fizzy orangeade and beer, nuts, glasses and jars of pickles.

We collected a soup plate at the door and as soon as we were seated the Sgts and Officers were there with jugs of tomato soup and bottle openers. I swopped my beer for two orangeades and in the course of the meal drank six of them, if not more, and came away with another emptied in my mug.

The main course was pork, turkey, sausage, roast and cream pots., peas and cauliflower, followed by quite a good pudding with a white sauce. The Sgts. and Officers were dashing hither and thither, many of them quite drunk but all in good humour. The RSM and CO didn't seem to serve much but signed menus, as did the others between times.

At the end the CO said a few words through the loudspeaker system installed for the purpose, thanked us all for our hard work etc and hoped we'd carry on with it after a nice Christmas break. After which we more or less broke up – (they passed the hat round for the cooks) – and as we left we filled our pockets with the nuts and sweets left on the table. I only drank fizz, but I feel quite dizzy so I don't know how the others must feel. Next stop buffet tea.

Well we heard the Queen on the radio and went straight to tea – should have gone half an hour earlier – most people had gone an hour before the proper time – shambles.

The jelly and blancmange had been put in large containers with trays of pies, sausages, ham and bread etc on a table down the middle of the hall. The first there had swiped loads, and the other tables were loaded with scraps of cakes, pies, plates of uneaten jelly and tinned fruit, mauled about and left by drunken pigs who didn't really want it. As a result we only got a little jelly and blancmange and a mug of tea. The place was in uproar and only two light bulbs worked in the hall.

Fortunately I don't feel particularly hungry, I have loads of sweets, some currants and some wine, so I'm not worried. The Naafi is sold out except for beer and is packed with a sullen mob still knocking it back. In my tent is a happier party of six, with little but the small drop of wine left but no inclination to drink it yet – just talk and the radio, quite a change – might even get an early night.

Boxing Day 1955

I woke about eight, too late for breakfast so I decided to stay in bed until Naafi time. Ted Hollands produced the tail end of his superb Christmas cake and some biscuits so we had a nibble and Tony, who usually makes the most mess and tidies up only at the point of a gun decided that for once he'd sweep up the mess on the floor, nut shells, toffee papers etc. and a few bits of glass. We'll have to take the matting up soon but I can't be bothered yet so it will have to wait until tomorrow or the weekend.

Well, as this is pretty well the end of Christmas and I've written twenty pages I will close and get this into the post, hoping it will give some impression of the goings on over the weekend.

View from my tent – Episkopi.

Episkopi, 14th January 1956

Passport arrived safely yesterday.

I've put in for leave in February to go to Jerusalem about the 6th – 19th February.

I hope the riots settle down or I will not be able to go. Next job, Visas.

... Pretty cold here at times in the dark hours especially, but quite hot sun at other times.

Just off night shift.

The other morning I saw a very rare sight. A dark cloud area behind the Signal Centre, as we looked across the valley, contrasted strongly with a brilliant rainbow, then an outer rainbow appeared and finally I noticed that the inner one was a V shape and I found, when I looked across the RAF camp towards the peninsular that the sun, low over the sea, was so brilliantly reflected on the dead flat of the water that the reflected light gave off its own rainbow and we could see the two where they did not quite coincide.

Episkopi, 23rd January 1956

... Two of the troop announced their intention of going down to Limassol and I joined them and we made up a party of five in all. Two of us wore civvies but the others wore uniform so they had to take a Sten gun. We started about eight and by chance caught a late bus to town. At 1/- a head this was even better than hitching a truck for the sixteen miles.

The drive took us along the top of the cliffs at the head of the flat peninsular then down to the plain. There we passed the fields of Carob trees, a few olives here and there, and the grey-green floor of the groves slashed across by the deep red-brown patches of ploughed soil. Two oxen, rather golden brown ones, were pulling a wooden plough past a bright yellow tractor parked in a field. The general colour throughout was this grey green which forms the perfect foil for the white, red-roofed buildings and the occasional patch of ploughed land. The far hills, grey-blue, rising beyond, and the sky somewhat threatening in spite of the brilliant sun.

In the town, of course, I seemed back in Palma, the stucco buildings, the lovely wrought iron in all sorts of places, windows, balconies, even on the most ramshackle houses. The red-orange "Roman tiled" roofs, the "entrada" or courtyard room inside the street door, with tiled floor, potted plants, staircase, the holy pictures; narrow cobbled streets, overloaded barrows, and bikes at all points along the kerb making the many pedestrians skip in and out of the honking traffic and causing congestion in shop doorways – shoppers and shelterers!

We had been dropped by the bus a little short of the sea front, outside a large and beautiful domed church – Greek Orthodox, complete with a Greek flag outside. We made first for the sea as I knew there I would find out about a ship for my leave. With my immediate problem settled, we began to search for a means of travel for three of the others who hope to visit Turkey in July.

So we progressed along the sea front. The sea wall is flush with the road surface, a broad walk planted recently with a line of young trees. The crystal sea lapped some six feet below us as we looked out at the ships moored some two or three hundred yards off. Small wooden jetties or piers at intervals, the only breaks in the sweep from the small stone quay on our right to the rolling slopes of the bay receding into the distance on our left.

Quite some way along the front we reached a recommended café-restaurant just as we needed a lemonade, and we decided to go back there for dinner.

First, to look for the Passport Office. I seemed to be leading most of the time as the others dithered somewhat, and with the apprehensions about being shot at and so on it was an odd sensation. I think, quite honestly that the Sten would have taken our "escort" five whole minutes to get into action, but of course it was never called for. We were directed by an agency to a building opposite the GPO, so made for one with a clock. I saw from notices outside that it was the Town Hall, but the others walked in and asked for the "Consulate".

Dinner. Back in the clean bright little café we were the only customers. The bar at the back carried the whole range of drink available in the island and two of us had a vermouth while waiting for the meal to be cooked. This, predictably, went straight to my head and I felt a bit dizzy for the rest of the meal.

Then our meal arrived, and such a meal! A steak almost the size of the envelope on this letter, a clean fried egg (the operative word is clean), chips, peas, and a slice of fresh tomato. A large, long roll and a generous pat of butter and all for the reasonable sum of five shillings. We ordered coffee afterwards, "dolly tea cups" full of the strongest, sweetest explanation for the glass of water given with it you could get anywhere. Delicious, anyway, and it steadied me back to normal – as you might say.

Episkopi, 7th February 1956

Today we got up about dinner time,(after night shift) and went down to Limassol to visit the KEO wines, spirits and beer factory, A most pleasant outing for the shift, with Mr. Blair, half of us in civvies.

We were first given a bottle of a sort of coca-cola while we watched it being bottled, then through to the bottle wash and along to a wine bottling plant. No tasters here but we were given small sample bottles of various wines and spirits.

Then up into an enormous high building – not yet completed, one of the most modern breweries in the world I should think. The ice rooms where the beer is fermented and stored – the lovely copper vats running from floor to ceiling, gleaming shapes in white tiled rooms. We climbed to the very top floor just to be shown a small grey "barley crusher" which sends the powdered barley down chutes into the vats and boilers.

From a window I had a wonderful view of the landscape inland, rising to the blue hills, clouded today as it was rather rainy. And below lay more empty bottles than I could ever imagine. They were all neatly stacked and sorted into green and brown mounds, very regular and "squared off". About fifty bottles – (I counted) end to end, the base about 14 ft wide and the mound a good five feet to the flat top. There were at least a dozen of these mounds.

Some of the party had really come for the free drinks, so they were pretty impatient by the time we eventually emerged onto a terrace roof and crates of beer and a tray of sandwiches appeared. There was

Letters Home ~ 43

more beer than they could drink in the time, and it was impossible to take any away. I had none, but I managed to get three of the sandwiches. I had almost forgotten that bread can be enjoyed for itself and this rather rough bread and the delicious cheese have made me even more aware of the tastelessness of the stuff dished out by the RASC bakeries.

With a final flourish we were offered tasters of a not very good creme de menthe and we made our way back to the truck. It was getting cold and dull by that time and the canvas roof was closed in, except at the bit where I was.

This was fortunate, as the schools had turned out, and as we passed a village a mob of children suddenly let fly and an enormous shower of stones rattled and thudded against the truck. At my open space I felt rather vulnerable but their aim was bad so I have no war wounds as yet! We are not only on Active Service and all that but have actually been under fire from local riotous mobs or whatever the papers call them!

Episkopi, 9th February 1956

...I've decided that my wind jacket is too thin for Jordan so I may get a jacket in Limassol next week. Have got passport type photos for my visa applications.

... It has rained fitfully for three or four days now, terrific wind-rain-hail squalls which saturate the tents and make life rather cold and damp. My oil stove is one of the few still working in our tent line and we huddle over it and try to dry things with that and the iron.

I don't know the force of the winds but I've never experienced anything like it and we wonder if the tent is about to leave us at any moment. The hillside is laced with torrents of water which flood across the paths and form a new river at the bottom, which pours out to the sea, a fierce swirl of red muddy water streaked with the rainbow of oil film. Everything is squelchy mud off the paths of concrete and these paths are awash where a blockage in a gutter deflects the racing water.

I hope the wind will die down before I put to sea next week. The sea, from our high viewpoint, is flecked with foam to the horizon and great breakers roll in to the beach. The Med. is usually so calm too.

Episkopi, 14th February 1956

... Latest gen. on leave plans.

I went to Limassol yesterday to check on the boat and get my Passport endorsed for travel in the Arab states. The DSO at Nicosia told me on the 'phone that this had to be done and he has sent visa forms for me to fill in and sign so that he can get the visas for me.

I found that there is no ship this Saturday after all so my dates are put back a week again and the new sailing date is 25th and when I enquired about return dates, of which there is no mention in the timetable, I found that there are no ships of any kind doing the Beirut to Cyprus trip except via Port Said! The only way back is by air. This is a blow as no one who has made the trip had warned me of this. I can still cover the expenses but it's a bit tight and not the comfortable financial position I had expected. The single fare back from Beirut to Nicosia will be £8 in stead of a £2 boat fare.

With £16 loaned from Pop and £16 savings in hand here to cover the trip, I took the other cash I have saved to look for civvies when we were in Limassol.

Most shops will make suits etc. in a few days but do not carry stocks of ready-mades, so I tried lots before finding one that did. He had a ghastly sports jacket in the doorway of the open front shop, and on the wall hung an assortment of suits, mainly bluish ones. I asked about jackets and tried the sports jacket for politeness as I hoped he had others. Then I tried a suit jacket and liked the material and finish, but not the fit. The next one might have been made for me, and the others with me all liked it so I considered it a "possible". The trousers were not so hot but he wanted £4.10/- for the jacket and the trousers were optional at £2 extra, and peg bottoms. Then I spotted a pair of gabardine slacks, almost the same tone but a bit lighter and greyer so we measured them up and they matched my measurements near enough and I got them for 30/-.

My escort, at the door with the Sten all this time, approved of the outfit and so that part of my complicated arrangements has been dealt with.

Well, as we were all broke after that, we started looking for transport back to camp. Just then a Signals truck came by with the Sqdn Office clerks with Stens in the back, so I hailed them and we all got a lift.

Today it went on Orders that Limassol is "Out of Bounds" – so I only just managed it in time!

... "The Authorities" have just taken it into their heads to send a party of Cypriots round the lines to extend the concrete floors by about a foot all round. This stretches the tent walls to the limit and of course the roof is still the same size, a bit small now for the base. The idea is to give us more room when we push the things back to the wall. I suppose it will but the difficulty of fixing the bottom of the wall in a high wind is increased by the stretch. Just waiting for a rain storm to try us out. I scrounged a bit of cement to fill in the cracks in the floor, so that's something.

Episkopi, 17th February 1956

... The DSO Nicosia, Mr. Black, has been most helpful ... We had a long telephone conversation about my leave plans at 3 am the other night and the visa forms and Passport went back to him by SDS in the morning. Today he rang up for travel dates and we sent a DSO Log over the radio circuit, and several unofficial logs on the subject passed over circuit to clear matters. – Hope the circuit wasn't being monitored!

Episkopi, 21st February 1956

... Passport arrived back from Nicosia this morning. I had applied in Limassol for endorsements for Syria, Lebanon and Jordan to get to Jerusalem, but the Official there had just put "Jerusalem" and stamped it. Apparently, as this is " no known State" it is quite useless and Mr. Black had to go and get it properly endorsed before he could get me the visas!

... I start leave at 6 pm (after shift) Thursday. This gives me Friday to pack etc and get down to Limassol, I hope, for boat ticket and so on.

...Note added on shift. Visas for Syria and Lebanon safe, must get Jordan en route and return ones on way back. Cost so far 12/6d. Jordan will be about £1.

Not much to add. Rough night. Lots of work, glad it's my last night shift for a couple of weeks.

Dog handler got mauled by his guard dog outside. Messy. Hands mainly.

Episkopi, 24th February 1956

Final note before the great trek begins.

Today I got the boat ticket for tomorrow, and paid for the 'plane ticket which I must collect tomorrow. The boat sails about 4 pm so we should see quite a bit of the coast before it gets dark at 6.

I found a chap who'd hired a car and was going in to Limassol and he gave a lift to myself and a friend who was to get out a hired car also. My luck being true to recent form, the radiator burst half way and we were stuck for an hour while the driver got a lift in to town and returned with the owner in another car. Then we got into the second car and continued.

The boat cost £2 plus 17/- Port Tax after all. The 'plane just £8 so far, I don't know if they'll charge extra fees for landing! I arrive in Beirut at 8 or 9 pm and then the real fun begins. It's half Moslem and half Christian there and they speak Arabic and French. I must get a Taxi to start my trip, or get Visas for Jordan, or find a hotel – I don't know yet! Not to worry!

Well, I tried all afternoon to get Unit Transport to the boat tomorrow, with no result so far. Mr. Blair may fix something but if not, I'm going with him at 9 am to collect my 'plane ticket (he's to hire a car – everyone hires cars!) and if necessary I'll stay there, though he is not keen to leave me alone and unarmed as Security Orders say I should carry at least a pistol, or "go in fours" or be in uniform in twos with Stens, – still, as they are letting me go solo to Jerusalem I think it's a queer state of affairs.

I have been loaned a suitcase and a Pac-a-mac by two friends and have packed a few sweets and biscuits for the trip. My army pullover is ready for wear at the top of the case, and my sketch board and paper at the bottom, in the hope that I'll get the chance to use the paints and ink also packed.

I've got £15 in Travellers Cheques, £5 in Sterling notes, and £4 in Cyprus notes, so I hope that will be enough.

RAF Camp, Amman, Hashemite Kingdom of Jordan, Sunday 26th February 1956

Well I'm rather tired but I must write before any more impressions crowd in on me.

Mr. Blair dropped me in Limassol, alone and unarmed, at about 10.30 am and drove away wishing me the best of luck but looking very worried as he did so. I must write tomorrow and set his mind at rest.

There I was on the sea front of Limassol, where all other troops move in twos or threes armed to the teeth. I collected my 'plane ticket and walked along to the Shipping Office, where I left my case and strolled back along the front for a meal.

I passed Delices half way along, as everyone goes there, and went to the far end, to the place where I had enjoyed a meal before. Had a superb meal of liver, chips, peas, salad and fried egg for 5/-, then back to the Shipping Office for the great wait.

Nothing to do until about 3 pm and the town completely out of bounds from 1 pm.

I watched the other passengers who popped in to leave bags etc. and was especially curious about five young Cypriots, all about 20 and each with an enormous new case. One, who appeared their leader, was quite a latin Tony Curtis, with brown curly hair. More of them later.

The ship was now not sailing at 4 but 6 pm., and I should be aboard by 5. So at three I got fed up with the Office and walked along to the Customs. There, outside closed doors an enormous crowd of friends and relatives were greeting or parting from the travellers popping into or out of the doors when they opened momentarily every so often.

I stood well back to get the hang of it all, and when Police moved in to the crowd and a woman had a screaming fit, the crowd became quite excited and I had visions of a Briton stoning riot – but it was just that a woman had had a child by a man who had now come back from abroad, not to marry her, but to bring his wife!

Fascinating, but I was unable to find out if it was the wife or the other woman who had the fit of screaming!

The crowd thinned a little near one door, so I edged forward and almost became involved in a Greek (or was it Turkish?) family parting. The small boys kissed Daddy's hand, then suddenly Mother, and Granma collapsed in tears on his shoulder and the boys and their sister, aged about eight, looked from one to another as Father fought bravely not to join in. I found it too much and edged away with a big lump in my throat.

There was another rush as a door opened and again I was still some way from it. Then I noticed two obviously-on-leave-from-the-army types and we joined forces and got in at the next chance. Inside, a spacious hall with a few benches for baggage inspection, and away in a far corner a mass of people fighting to get their Passports stamped at a desk.

We stood about and nobody took any notice. So we chose a man with two gold rings on his cuff and he took our Passports to the back of the bench and got us seen to in no time. Then we asked about baggage and he said, well, if we liked, and called across a civilian with a piece of chalk.

This chap asked if we had radios or ammunition, laughed when we said no, and made a squiggle on the bags.

So, in a little motor boat we went out to the ship and clambered up the ladder to the deck. At once our tickets and Passports were taken from us and we just drifted about the deck, uncertain what to do. A deck hand gave us deck chairs, but after three moves out of the way of various loading and unloading operations we abandoned them.

The sailing time was put back at intervals owing to loading delays so we didn't sail until 9 pm after all – or was it 10? Anyway at about 8 we enquired from the office agent who had come aboard. He took us right up to the bow where a cramped little dining room is fitted for the 3rd and 4th class passengers (we were 4th).

By this time we had lost one of our number to a party of Syrians who got him drunk on brandy, and we had added in his place the M.O. from the Royal Norfolk's who was bound for a skiing holiday at the Cedars in Lebanon.

We saw the food offered, not good, and asked the price. They said we could have a meal for 5/- if we came back in 15 minutes.

Well, the Doctor went for a scout around and left the two of us.

Suddenly I was approached by my latin Tony Curtis who asked if I would forgive him if he asked me something, so I said, please do. He had heard us told the meal would be 5/-. He had just eaten the meal and it was not worth it. Also he was Turkish and it was a Greek ship and they were bound for London and had brought some food with them and did not need it all, so would we like to come to his cabin and have some food there!

This really was something, so I said, yes please for both of us and he and another with him were highly delighted and led the way. Right next to the 3rd class dining room was a tiny cabin with 6 bunks, and we were made to sit on two bunks while they produced two hard boiled eggs for each of us, an orange, a tangerine, and a supply of rusk-like rolls, ideal for taking on a journey as they don't get stale – seeds on top too. Also a salty Cypriot cheese which they did not expect us to like but it was there if we wanted it – so I tried a little.

They explained that three Turks and two Greeks were going to England to work. They have been encouraged by Army Officers now back in UK and have little or no intention of returning to Cyprus – the Turks would rather go to relations in Istanbul. Two are to join the Fire Brigade at Harwich as they were in the Fire Service at Famagusta.

Anyway, the Greeks we did not really meet, but the Turks were wonderful. When they found we were on deck all night they opened their cases to reveal brand new blankets which they loaned us for the night. Then they insisted on providing more eggs, oranges and rolls for breakfast. All because we were British on leave and they were Turkish!

It was chilly on deck chairs overnight but we kept out of the wind and about 6 am we were watching the sun rise over the snow-clad mountains on the horizon. Soon Beirut was visible, a strange shape looming out of the mist at the foot of the first range of hills.

(must condense the rest as I want to get to bed)

It took ages to get ashore, Customs again only asked about wireless and ammo. The others were to stay in Beirut so I looked about for taxi. Found party of three already haggling for taxi to Jerusalem. Wanted £4 a head. No go. I wanted 30/-. However another taxi finally agreed for £2, expecting to save Beirut Hotels etc. Then, outside Beirut, another discussion and we found we were only getting to Amman. As that took until 8.30 pm it's far enough.

American, two Arabs and me. American spoke Arabic perfectly and Arabs spoke Spanish so I got on. Big yankee car. So, up and up, a wonderful climb above Beirut, fantastic view, right up to and above snow level, – only patches where we were.

Lovely sunny morning. Passport check, Customs further along road. Then a stone marking frontier, and another Customs, then Passport check – and we were in Syria.

The detail of it all blurs and I think it was then that we crossed the great plain to the foot of another range of mountains. On top of this one the final Syrian Customs, and on the way down a sign post for the frontier mark – made obvious by the abrupt end of the tarmac road of Syria where it meets the dust and stones of the rutted track into Jordan. This extends (apart from the towns) to the bridge over the River Jordan, where the old Palestine border was. There begins a good road to Jerusalem.

Forgot to mention modern town of Damascus in Syria, where we changed cars. I got my Jordan Visa at the border office (£1) and have only my return transits for Syria and Lebanon to get now – should be OK having got one way already.

Drive through darkness to Amman, a web of lights sprinkled on a cluster of hills dark in the moonlight. Alighted there.

The others made off and an Arab boy was impatient with my case and I landed at the Continentale Hotel where they wanted 30/- for the night, so I got them to get a taxi and I came here to the RAF for 2/6d, booked in at the Guard Room.

Orderly Sgt. found a bed in a little room one end of a billet, issued with bedding on signature, supper in the Naafi, and I'll continue to Jerusalem in the morning.

Cheers for the RAF, now bed.

Casa Nova Hostal, Old City, Jerusalem, 27th February 1956

This morning I left the RAF at Amman and got into the town in time for the 8 am taxi/bus service run by the Petra service, 7/- for the 2 hour run. Down and down the hairpin twisting road, past the Sea Level sign into the plain of the Dead Sea, which lay to our left. I thought at first the plain was flat but it was like a new mattress, and cut about by sharp dips in the barren mounds. So, across the Bailey bridge over the Jordan and on to Jericho, where I noticed that the Arab women's dresses were not the usual plain black ones but striped with bright embroideries and with heavily decorated bodices.

The area beyond the town is a mass of huts where some 40,000 refugees live, a fantastic sight. Then suddenly we dived between two steep hills and began the tortuous climb up past sea level and on up. At last I spotted a church tower on the far hills and guessed that Jerusalem was now near. Through Bethany and on up and up until quite suddenly we came abreast of the Holy City, riding like a great ship on the next hill beside us.

Down, past the Church of All Nations at the Garden of Gethsemene and up along the wall to Herod's Gate, where I got another taxi round the city wall to a back gate, the Dung Gate, and then in, and finally on foot to the Casa Nova, where the Warden had a grand argument with the boy who carried my case as I had only offered 6d and he wanted 1/-. So I gave him 1/- to save argument.

I have a neat little room to myself, and the bed looks most inviting. Thick soft carpet on the floor, wash basin with running cold water by the window, – window on to the inner court unfortunately.

At lunch I met the seven or eight other guests (very few visitors in the town at present, luckily) There are two elderly French ladies and a number of Priests of various nationalities, French and Spanish of sorts, and an extremely helpful RAF Officer who may move on tomorrow. After lunch he took me on a lightning tour of "the lot", apart from the Mosque on the site of the Temple. I have been to the Holy Sepulchre; Calvary; Via Dolorosa; and a whole host of Churches; the Convent -where the original courtyard of the Palace – where the trial was held – is preserved in the basement. We went to the Garden of Gethsemene; up the Mount of Olives to the spot of the Ascension, where an all-religion mosque/church area is walled off.

The view from here, the highest spot, is superb, although it was a dull day.

We only tipped a Guide at this place, because it is run by Moslems. Elsewhere we shook off Arabs and Orthodox chappies but put something in the Franciscans' plates as they ask for nothing. Now I am all set for a leisurely tour of these places again and hope to draw around the place during the week. I'll fire off the black and white film in the camera and get the colour one loaded in case the sun comes through the grey sky.

We also went to the Pool of Bethsida. I think it was where the Angel disturbed the water and the first in was made whole, or something. On a wall was the appropriate text in all languages – even Chaldean, but I don't think they get many visitors from there now!

Coming up the Via Dolorosa we met a funeral coming down. First, a man carrying the coffin lid, then banners and acolytes, then a Franciscan Priest, followed by the dead man himself laid in state in his best suit, socks and fez in the open coffin. And behind a great crowd of men in brown and black suits.

There's no knowing what will pop up next on this trip!

Casa Nova Hostal, Old City, Jerusalem, 28th February, 1956

Today Chris (RAF) and I got up at 6 am and went to the Holy Sepulchre Church for Mass. Mass had finished at Calvary so we went to the next one, a low Mass with sung responses at the Tomb itself.

Under the great dome stands the Tomb, like a building within a building. The Tomb was originally in the hillside, and the antechamber, and the surrounding hill rock was dug away to leave the Tomb clear. Then an ornate antechamber was built, and the Tomb itself overlaid with marble, which has been replaced at various times.

However, that is the spot. Mass is said on the slab and there is just room for the feet when one kneels at this altar. Only the Priest and his Server are there.

Outside, under the dome we sat on wooden benches to one side. The choir of six Franciscans stood opposite the entrance. When they sang they were answered by a choir of Arab-voiced boys in a chapel in the side of the Church, which is a mass of supporting girders and crumbling masonry. The organist got his cue from the Server, a bearded monk who came to the door and rang a bell.

A Verger asked us if we wanted Communion and when it was time we were beckoned into the antechamber to kneel at the pedestal containing a piece of the original round stone from the door. The Priest bent very low to come through the tiny opening from the tomb. His Latin was delivered with a marked Spanish accent.

After Mass we split up and wandered about the Church. I revisited the place where the Cross was discovered (probably in a dyke against Hadrian's wall, or a cave, somewhere convenient for dumping before the Sabbath)

Then back for breakfast, coffee, eggs and bread and jam. Afterwards off to the French Embassy for Chris to make some enquiries. On the way back we visited the Dominican Church, the Anglican Cathedral, and Gordon's "Garden Tomb", where, about 1860, an attempt was made to reveal the True Site of the Calvary and Tomb, which had apparently been mistaken by Christians until that date! It's an awful long way from the site of the Trial, where the Way of the Cross begins, so the Cross would have taken a bit of carrying there. It is now a horrid rockery garden where one expects to see a fishing gnome at any moment – there *is* a bird bath!

We went into the Tombs of the Kings of Jordan a very interesting place, where tombs of the kind used in Christ's time are preserved, even to the rolling stone. Down past the stone, through a small doorway we clambered into a large antechamber off which led the tombs, and passing into further antechambers we inspected tomb after tomb and descended eerie holes to further tombs at quite a depth. The best had these same shelves cut in the wall of rock, on which the bodies would simply have laid. A small niche for a lamp was cut at the back of each.

Some tombs were just long spaces opening back from the antechamber, about 2 ft high. I presume the body would go in head or feet first and that was that.

Anyway, the genuine article.

Back for lunch, having bought some cards. Afterwards, Chris decided to leave for Letroun Monastery before his Bill at the Casa Nova got any bigger, so he packed and left. He has shown me most of the things I should see and been very helpful.

Now, apart from the two Wardens, I have only French and Spanish conversations left!

I got on pretty well with one of the French ladies – I met her as I was out using the camera later this afternoon. She was walking to the Mount of Olives so we went as far as the Garden of Gethsemene together. The sky was patchy, bright sun and cloud, so I had to wait for the right moments. Later it rained a bit so I was glad of the mac.

Casa Nova Hostal, Old City, Jerusalem, 1st March 1956

Today I got up at the frightful hour of 5.30 and went down to St. Sepulchre for Mass. Here everyone goes to bed at about eight or nine and gets up early so I have no difficulty doing the same.

I had asked the Chilean Priest what time he would say Mass but he said it depended on what time an Altar was free, there are so many Priests wishing to use the Altars they take turns one after another. However, as I arrived he appeared at the Altar of the Crucifixion, on the believed spot of the actual Nailing to the Cross. There were some Nuns and a few convent school girls there also.

The Warden had arranged a Guide for me, for £1 for the day, and at 8.30 we set off for the Mosques on the site of the great Temple, which occupies about one sixth of the area within the city walls. Entrance ticket-cum-booklet cost another 5/- but it was worth it although it was raining and I couldn't use the camera.

I'm told this is second only to Mecca in importance to Moslems and the main circular domed Mosque is over the rock where the Holy of Holies was and David saw the Avenging Angel, as well as being the spot where Mohammed rose to heaven on his horse, etc. etc. This rock is exposed in the centre as an irregular mound surrounded by a pierced rail. The Rock of the Agony is exposed in a similar way in the Church of the Agony or Church of All Nations as it is called.

Letters Home ~ 55

We visited the Mosque Al- Aqsa, which closely resembles a Christian Basilica, and is the place where King Hussein's father (or grandfather?) was assassinated. Thence to the Wailing Wall, the last fragment of Herod's Temple, and, I gather, the most precious fragment of anything left to the Jews anywhere, but since "the trouble" they don't have access to it. It is extraordinary to look across to the next hill and think, that is Israel, and the Arabs are always in fear of attack from there.

Next we took a bus from Damascus Gate (I asked for the cheapest means) to Bethany, to the new Franciscan Church dedicated to Martha, Mary , and Lazarus.

Fragments of ancient mosaics from earlier churches are preserved under trap doors in the courtyard and can be inspected.

So back through the rain for lunch, after which we shared a taxi for the longish ride to Bethlehem. A new road has had to be built as the old one cuts across Jewish territory. So it takes a little longer now. A wonderful ride, except for the rain, past the domed Tomb of Rachel to the town and through the narrow streets to the Church of the Nativity with its tiny main door, almost blocked up and about four feet high – for mediaeval defence -(the eye of a needle). Through this into a basilica whose columns still bear Crusader paintings. Beneath trapdoors, the ancient floor is revealed some 18 ins. below the present one – they charged me 1/- to open the lid!

Avoiding the High Altar, which is Greek, and very ugly we went to the steps at the side which lead down under the Altar to the Grotto.

Here, beneath the little Greek Orthodox Altar is the Catholic Star of Bethlehem, bearing a Latin inscription to say that this is the spot where Jesus was born. Following tradition, I placed the small crosses I have bought for the nieces and nephews in the centre hollow of the Star and again on the site of the Manger, a Franciscan shrine opposite. Also in the crypt or grotto are Altars to the Innocents, St. Jerome, and others.

Then, to the Church of St. Catherine, alongside, the Franciscan Church from which Midnight Mass is broadcast, and whence the Child statue is carried in procession to the Manger.

So back to the Casa Nova, having had a busy day already, where I removed my soaking wet shoes and sat down for a bit, then suddenly got the idea to take the crosses I had been touching on Holy Places to the Holy Sepulchre and get them blessed in the special manner for Indulgences. As I opened my door the little French lady opposite came out , and seeing me, asked if I was just going for a walk, or going to the Procession. I asked what Procession and off we went together.

At 4 pm daily, the Franciscans hold a Procession all round the Holy Sepulchre Church, and we joined this, armed with tapers and Latin texts. It was most impressive, much of it sung, in plain chant, each stop finishing with Our Father, Hail Mary, and Glory be; down the steps to the Chapel of St. Helena; down to the Finding of the Cross; up to Calvary and down again to the Stone of the Anointing; and so to the Tomb. Then the spot where Christ appeared to Mary in the garden and finally the Litany of the B.V. Mary in the Franciscan Chapel of the Apparition, where, afterwards, I got my oddments blessed.

Then having wandered back here with my French lady I had a little excursion to find the Citadel, and on my return counted up my remaining cash to estimate what I could manage and went to the little shop next door to find some little gifts to send home.

Casa Nova Hostal, Old City, Jerusalem, Friday 2nd March 1956

Got up at 5.30 am again today and went down to the Holy Sepulchre to see what Masses were going on. As I got to the top of the steps to Calvary one of the Altar boys was just pointing his finger at all present to ask if they wanted Communion – he spotted me afar off so I nodded and joined the Mass at the Altar of the Nailing to the Cross without further delay. Then back to breakfast. The French ladies had been enthusing about a Solemn High Mass to be at the Chapel of the Condemnation, which stands on the Lithostrotos, or pavement of the Palace courtyard where the trial took place and Pilate washed his hands. Part of the floor is the original rutted stone. So I went with them, or rather, caught up with them on the way.

I next made my way out of the Damascus Gate to enquire at the Petra office, and booked my seat in various cars all the way to Beirut, starting at 7 am and arriving in the evening, same day. All for 170 Piastres or £1. 14/-, pretty good.

Then I went to the Palestine Archeological Museum. It is outside the walls, opposite the Herod Gate. On Fridays it is 2 Piastres (6d) in stead of the usual 10, so of course, being also the Arab Sabbath there were school parties going round. I greatly enjoyed the place, it is well set out and is supposed to be one of the best in the Middle East.

I drew some bronze age pots from Jericho, BC 1200 – 1600-ish. This amused and amazed the Arab school boys who also tried out their English on me. A Warden commented I was a "good drawer" when he saw the terra-cotta bull I had done, and I also noted a Byzantine cut copper medallion which will possibly be my Christmas card next year.

After lunch I popped off on a "touching tour" with the crucifix and a string of Jerusalem crosses for distribution, and ended up at the Franciscan chapel for the special blessing. Out came the Priest whose Latin had convinced me he was Spanish. When I asked for ten of the little certificates they sign and give with the blessing he counted them in Spanish so I thanked him in Spanish, which amused him.

Every Friday, at 3 pm, the Franciscans hold a Procession in the streets to visit the Stations of the Cross but owing to the weather, this week the Stations were held in St. Saviour's Church. It has rained all day and my shoes are quite sodden. Afterwards my indefatigable French lady offered to show me the family Tomb of Joseph of Arimathea, as she had her torch with her today. So back to the Sepulchre and through a door leading out of the rotunda behind the Sepulchre itself. Through a little Chapel we passed into a low tomb like the ones I have described before, carved in the solid rock.

I had announced my intention of visiting Gethsemene again but first I had to be shown the Bazaar, the Souk, a fantastic covered series of alleys with open shops selling all sorts of wares which bulged forth into the pathway, each with its murderous looking shopkeeper and also numerous peddlers. My friend babbled away in French and we were, I'm sure, the only Europeans in the place.

The Jewish Quarter, and all the Jewish Cemeteries have been so horribly desecrated that I hate to think what they might want to do to the Muslims if they start attacking the Old City again. The gossip is flying about, though I understand very little, and perhaps it is as well that I leave on Monday. British prestige is not doing too well, I gather.

I have noticed a number of Americans but only – I think – two English people (tourists) in five days walking about the city – Oh yes there was that terribly English -looking Ecclesiast, all in mauve in the courtyard of the Anglican Cathedral outside the walls, but he's not visiting, he's the Bishop.

I made my way, alone, through the pouring rain to Gethsemene, and sheltered in the garden gateway and watched the rain on the Olives. Then back to the Casa Nova where I settled down to write all this, pausing only for dinner. I think I drank a little too much wine. An hilarious conversation in French and Spanish finally became too much for me and I withdrew. I have got on very well with the two French ladies and the Spanish-speaking Priests who all explain odd words in English, so I suspect they know more than they will use if they can help it.

Now I must get some old newspapers from the Warden to stuff my shoes, then bed.

Casa Nova Hostal, Old City, Jerusalem, Saturday 3rd March 1956

Again it was a rainy day, but with time running out I pressed on regardless and walked all the way down to the St. Stephen Gate and out to the Garden of Gethsemene. I've wanted to "do an Olive" all the week but the weather has let me down. Rather than give up entirely though,

I made a small drawing, in pencil, of one of the trees, while I sheltered in the porch of the Sacristy.

As I finished, it stopped raining and there I was, sunlight, and no camera!

I dashed all the way back for it and between showers and dull patches managed to utilise the three-minute bursts of sunshine to use up a little more of the colour film.

So, wet, back to dinner – beefsteak and rice, with, or followed by salad, soup before and an orange and coffee after. Wine with the meal as usual, so I laid down for a bit afterwards.

Then I went down to the Sepulchre with the idea of trying to get above the Tomb somewhere – can't be done – and arrived there just as they were preparing to receive the Patriarch himself in all his glory of pale cyclamen and white fur.

The Procession was again made round the Holy Places, loads of singing, then three times round the rotunda and Litany of the B.V. in the Franciscan Church, very well sung in polyphonic arrangement by answering choirs of men and boys.

... An Australian Priest arrived this afternoon so he monopolised my conversation at dinner, could be quite a bore when he gets going, I should think. However, he and the other Priests found they had Italian in common so I passed him on.

... I don't like the Greek Orthodox Priests and Religious, so unlike the Franciscans. They have a trick of standing by a collection plate and when a suitable tourist approaches they slip a couple of notes in the plate to make it appear the correct thing to do to leave something similar. They're an unkept lot, resembling the ancient Pharisees somehow, are always on the cadge for "something for the Church" which almost certainly goes into their own pockets to support their families. The youngest one at St. Sepulchre is a shifty eyed specimen with lank hair and a crafty expression.

... The Copts have their own little Chapel immediately behind the Tomb, on the same "island" in the middle of the Rotunda. They held their Service at the same time as the Procession today - (the Procession, with its four mace-stomping leaders, moved right through it undaunted). Their chant, extremely like Flamenco, rose in the pauses and was drowned in the swell of the plain chant of the procession.

These Procession leaders wear the Fez and black overcoats with bright red collars and a belt at the back to match. They carry great curved swords in decorated sheaths as well as the heavy silver-topped metal-tipped maces which they crash to the stone floor every three paces or so, an odd dead-slow rhythm. They also led the funeral we met.

Before them, two helmeted Arab Policemen – in khaki, and behind, the tiny boys from the orphanage in navy capes followed by the choir boys in scarlet capes and cassocks with white lace to the thighs. The exact order escapes me, but somewhere the Monks followed in the two files, then Acolytes with the Cross Bearer in between, and the Patriarch himself, with trainbearer, and escorted by two important looking Monks in smaller trainless capes of purple and sheepskin.

Garden of Gethsemane.

Casa Nova Hostal, Old City, Jerusalem, Sunday 4TH March 1956

Today we all went to 9 am High Mass in the Greek Catholic Rite, and most interesting too. I went to Communion about 6.30 then after breakfast had time to go down as far as St. Stephen's Gate for another couple of photos before joining the others to go to the Patriarchate Church. I wish I'd seen it before as it's a lovely little Church.

The singing, once you had got used to it, was very moving and I was unable to drag myself away before the end although I had told the others that as the sun was brilliant today I wanted to go drawing. Afterwards the two Spanish-speaking Priests and one French lady were going up Mount Olivet, so I collected my stuff and went with them.

At Gethsemene we met a Spanish Monk who opened the Garden for me and I stayed to draw while they went on up the hill. A convenient well-head made an ideal seat and I bashed away at an olive trunk. I was nowhere near finished when they came back at twelve so I had to rush and then leave it uncompleted after all.

Still, it's not bad, considering, and has saved me from complete disappointment in that direction. I could have done so much more if the sun had shone all the week.

I hurried up the hill into the Gate and up the Via Dolorosa to arrive just after 12.30 and join the others at dinner.

My elated state was evidently shared by all, and it was a lively meal. Afterwards the two Priests came to my room to inspect the Olive and my Pocket Book, which dated from March 7th '55 – just coming up to twelve months record of places seen. Then I almost dozed off and suddenly remembered I was to see Fr. Hugo at St. Sepulchre so I dashed off there and after a lightning tour of the Holy Places, asked for him at the Sacristy.

I was taken into a waiting room, and a Monk opened a cupboard to reveal a system of wires, buttons and lights. He pressed a button for Fr. Hugo and a bulb glowed softly. A moment later an answering bulb flashed on to say he was coming and after a few minutes he came hurrying to see me. We talked for nearly an hour until he had to lead the Procession held daily at four.

Tourist Hotel, Beirut, Lebanon, Monday 5th March 1956

With many regrets, of course, I have now returned to Beirut on the first stage of the trip back. I got my Visas at the Frontier, the Lebanese were a bit sticky as they said why did I think they have Consulates in Jerusalem and Amman if I couldn't bother use them. However, here I am.

I managed Mass and Communion at the Stabat Mater Altar, on the spot where Our Lady is supposed to have stood at the Crucifixion. On the Altar, in a glass case, is a life size statue, waist upwards of Mary with a jewelled sword piercing her heart.

Fr. Hugo said yesterday that a Muslim Guide was heard to tell a party of tourists that when this poor woman saw her son on the Cross she was so upset that she stabbed herself!

I dashed back for breakfast and was on my way by 6.35. At least three Arabs offered to carry my case for a piastre on the way and about twelve taxi drivers offered to take me to Amman or Damascus.

At last we were away and I had a good seat for my last glimpses of the city.

As we sped towards Jericho through the mountains I got far more of the impression that it was a desert. Down below sea level and out onto a more open road across the valley of the Dead Sea. At about 7.45 we were passing the refugee area and great crowds of children of all ages were doing arm swinging exercises outside two of the schools near the road.

After Jericho I looked for the Guards all along the road to the bridge but they were not there this time. The area here and especially after Amman is thick with Arab Legion camps.

In Amman, as everywhere in Jordan this week, every house, shop, and car was decorated with cloth or paper Jordanian flags and pictures of King Hussein, and coming out towards the edge of the town we passed about 200 school children and half a dozen Arab Legionaries moving along at a slow trot in time to a chanted song or slogan, waving arms and stamping feet while a Corporal strode backwards at their head, building up their excitement by waving his headdress in his hand. Just the sort of trouble making that makes Cyprus so difficult.

Out of the town I saw parties of these men on weapon training near their camps, mostly with rifles but some with mortars and field guns. There was shouting and merrymaking at the Damascus Gate last night too, with shots fired in the air – just as well I've evacuated, I really ought to read a newspaper and find out what it's all about. I know that someone named Glub Pasha has left the Legion, but that's all!

I wanted to write so much about the journey but arriving here just after 6 pm it has been quite a day and all my impressions have been confused. An Armenian who spoke fairly good English made the whole trip with me and as we were getting nearer here he began asking what sort of trip I was on, where from, and so on, and he told me he thought it was marvellous to make such a trip alone – so much so that he insisted he should show me where to change money and then showed me where this Hotel was,(after approving my choice as not expensive)

I'm four or five floors up in a room with two beds and a wash basin. Shower bath and lav. are next door – I've had a shower but it was cold, like the Army ones.

I'm hoping dinner will not be long as I've not eaten since breakfast.

I've got £2 (in local currency that is £16!) I walked round the shops and it's funny thinking of paying eight pounds for something worth only £1 Sterling, – the Livre here is roughly 2/6d English money.

Horrible thought – this time tomorrow I'll be back in Cyprus.

Waynes Keep Transit Camp, Nicosia, Wednesday 7th March 1956

The meal never materialised last night. The Manager "forgot all about it" he said, so I popped out at about 11 pm after waiting in the hope that it would appear even if late, and bought three hot dogs in a snack bar, in the main square of Beirut, catering for U.S. tastes.

This morning I paid for just the room – five and a half Lebanese pounds – and left without breakfast. I returned to the snack bar and had coffee and excellent rolls, softish milk-tasting ones with a fine light texture. I then found the office for my airline and left my bag.

I toured the surrounding streets for a couple of hours to pass the time and had Turkish coffee in the cleanest place I could find at about twelve. Then back slowly to the office to await the bus to the 'drome, through Customs etc. and another long wait, more coffee and a roll and a piece of cake, and then, at last, the 'plane.

Took off late, some time after three. Smooth flight, lovely views of Beirut and Cyprus. We taxied to a stop at the Customs, some 50 yards from the burnt out wreckage of the Hermes which exploded at the weekend. A terrorist bomb.

Horrible mess, the nose sticking sideways on its nosewheel, the wings tilted forward, resting on its engines propped up on oil drums, behind that, ashes, and then the fragments of a tail.

I found everything here Out of Bounds, so have been taken into protective custody at the Transit

Camp at Nicosia after waiting 2 hours for their truck. I've been issued with eating irons and blankets – no mattresses left, but it's only for one night.

A meal of egg, fish and fried bread, and a mug of tea.

I was lucky to get a tent with a light so I can write this. Working out the days I found my Troop should have been on afternoon shift today, so asked to use the 'phone about seven and managed to catch Mr. Blair before he went off shift.

He has not received the letter I wrote to him the day I got to Jerusalem.

Waynes Keep Transit Camp, Nicosia, Wednesday 7th March 1956

I'm stuck here until 2 pm so I may as well enlarge on yesterday's note.

The airways office in Beirut was on a main road leading up to a square with a big clock tower, so with this landmark I made fairly extensive tours of the streets, turnings and alleys leading off one another on either side, and wished I'd had some money to spend on the lace and the woollen shawls and clothes displayed in all manner of shops.

But, as I explained to the well dressed man who spoke to me on the seafront – he hadn't eaten for two days, was out of work and a refugee from Haifa and wanted me to buy him a sandwich – if I'd had the money to spare I'd have bought myself a sandwich too as I'd only had a few rolls and cups of coffee since leaving Jerusalem at 7 the previous morning!

I don't know how genuine his story was but it was only when I got to the Departure

Lounge and knew I had no Customs fees or Bus fares to pay for, that I dared break into my last Lebanese £5 note.

I bought a savoury roll and a piece of cake and three cups of coffee, which came

to 1 ½ pounds – a little over 3/-. The 'plane was two thirds empty and I got the seat in front of the wing quite easily as everyone else stayed at the rear. A smooth take off carried us towards the city from the airport which lies among sand dunes near the sea.

The road to the city runs straight through a thick plantation of pines whose bare trunks rose to some 40 feet to support a dense flat roof of dark green.

Beyond this belt of green the city spread from the sea to the foot of the mountains and as we turned seawards I could see the harbour at the north edge of the coastline. A last look at the snow-capped range and I settled down for just over half an hour of empty sea and sky before I glimpsed the pancake of cloud in the distance and under it the tip of Cyprus extending into the sunlight, the far mountains sticking blue into the lowest part of the cloud. Turning North to cross the coast we met the bumps and air pockets as we flew under the edge of the cloud towards Nicosia.

The Military at the Airport demanded to know the reason for my visit to Cyprus!

Episkopi, Wednesday 7th March 1956

Forty eight hours from Nicosia to here! I hung about at Waynes Keep until 2 pm and got the truck here without further problems. Four letters waiting for me...

I wish I could remember all the things that happened to me on the trip, the odd incidents – I even got stuck in a lift leaving the hotel in Beirut!

I drank coffee, sold by a man with a portable coffee maker and little china cups, high up on the Syrian border, and again in Beirut when a policeman who was talking to me invited me to have one. Lord! the coffee I consumed in Beirut, two for breakfast, another to while away the time, one with the Customs "cop" and three more at the airport when they gave me a great jug of coffee and one of milk.

...The pyjama clad man taking the air on a terrace roof just opposite my room in Beirut – 7am ... Have I told you how the two Arabs in the car on the way out sang Arab songs and clapped hands for mile after mile, and the wireless carried on for them between times... How I was left alone with the radio in Beirut and tuned in to Radio Cyprus to hear part of Beethoven's 5th Piano Conc., the first music other than Arab or Church music since leaving here.

...And the shoe shine boy on the sea front at Beirut, speaking perfect American who assured me "You British don't like going about in dirty shoes" when I refused to let him go to it on mine.

Episkopi, 25th March 1956

I'm writing this on Sunday, but as there is not going to be any Post in or out until Tues. or Wed. owing to the Emergency Situation at present I don't know when you'll get it. Everything is held up this weekend, no Post, no traffic on the roads, curfews all over the island and an EOKA attack on Episkopi expected at any moment. Guards are doubled and trebled here, and so on.

I'm Superintendent at the Sig. Office tonight and will have four men on shift. When we are closed down for the night we're to stand by with rifles in case any attack is made.

Meanwhile preparations for Admin. on Tuesday goes on. Only Signals are bothering this year!

Episkopi, 4th April 1956

... Tonight I'm Guard Commander for the first time. OK so far, 9.30 pm. 'Phone rings for all sorts of things, and the lights fused in the Regt. Armoury so I had to call in the Duty Electrician. Also a new intake arrived from UK and we had to see about a bed for him.

Hope nothing happens, as I have Sten and hardly a clue how to load or fire it!

Also seven rifles on my signature in case I have to call out the Security Picquet in a nearby tent. Only one man reporting for " Jankers" today and he's an old friend from my Troop anyway.

Episkopi, 10th April 1956

Now that the Admin. is over and accusations of needless "Bull" are less prevalent I've decided to enliven the soil in front of my tent with a little rock garden. I went along to the cliffs and collected loads of rock plants and a few tiny conifers, and with some 8in. or so chunks and slabs of weathered rock have made quite a difference to the 2 ft, of earth between the tent wall and the concrete path.

When we roll back the tent walls in the warmer weather it will be quite pleasant.

Letters Home ~ 67

Episkopi, 29th April 1956

... Today, Sunday, was our extra day off, while another shift does the 24 hrs., so we all went off on a trip to the Transmitter Site along the coast on a large plateau.

We first went to the sports grounds in "Happy Valley", a site near here which is being turned into a Sports Arena with a track and pitches for football, hockey and netball, all white dust, of course, no grass. After matches of hockey, netball and cricket had been played off against the TX Troop we were loaded into the trucks and we drove up out of the valley and over along the coast to a great sweeping plain where the land lay flat for great stretches, dotted with Olive and Carob trees whose ancient branches dipped to meet the full-grown wheat, which softened the bumps and hollows of the plain with an ever flowing shimmering surface of pale green.

Great rocky mounds stuck boldly up from the surface and beyond we could see one mound larger than the rest, topped by the silvery trellis of the radio masts.

CRE football pitch Episkopi.

The road edged up to this and cut through the steep front to emerge on the plateau and end finally on a little gravel square marked out for deck tennis.

When the second party arrived we were to have lunch, meanwhile, we all named our drinks at the bar and, refreshed, toured the great hall where the transmitters are housed, steel boxes with countless knobs and lights and a board to give the key to which box of tricks was involved with each of our Circuits. We had a special look at "Malta 2" the troublesome one.

Happy Valley – old house.

Then back to the dining-hut-cum-bar where lunch was unveiled and we were soon stuffing ourselves with egg, spam, and corned beef rolls, doughnuts and unlimited drinks. I stuck to Coke and Orange fizz all day, but while most people were reasonable a few spoilt things by drinking themselves unconscious – one of them, the driver – he lay on his back, out cold, all the way back while the stand-by driver drove.

After too many doughnuts for comfort I was introduced to deck tennis and we did quite well for a first attempt. The next pair, of our scheduled doubles matches, had had too much, and the games, darts and table tennis, all rather fell through from then on as no one in our party seemed very capable. The TX Troop had by this time given away the fact that the women on the shift were the real reason for the invitation, and I found several of our Troop got bored as they didn't want to drink and the other entertainments tailed off.

We all went down for a swim later and it was quite fun though the sea was running rather high and the rocky beach caused a few bruises. Again the drunks spoiled the fun for the others as they had to be carried back up the cliff having swigged brandy and Commanderia all the while they were on the beach. Silly isn't it.

So, back to camp about 5 ish as the shadows lengthened, to the task of tending the sick. Only Albert in our tent has had too much. He went flat out on his bed so I cleared the decks and put a bucket with a little water beside him. He found it and used it, so I emptied it and he used it again. I emptied it again and he is now in a deep sleep, past the stage of grunts and mumbles and banging his locker!

Episkopi, 30th April, 1956

... We reported for OC's this morning at 08.30 and were told to come back at 10.

So back to lie on the bed for a spell and then about fifty minutes waiting on the verandah.

At last L/Cpls Siddall and Hodges were marched in and the Charge read out that "whilst on Active Service we failed to report to a Place of Parade as detailed on Orders signed by the OC himself etc.etc" Sid had prepared lengthy excuses but I was asked to answer first and as I said simply I had failed to read Orders he was rather stumped and said " same as him". This, the OC pointed out was no excuse, but as I hadn't meant it to be I had no further comment.

Then he asked the SSM for our "sheets" and while Sid's was a two page effort, written on both sides, mine, when produced was blank apart from my name and number at the top. This impressed him and he asked how long I'd been "In", so I told him I had ten weeks left and he decided not to make too much of a mess.

So he admonished me with the warning that he doesn't want to see me before I go home and "if you're charged again within three months this charge will be taken into account".

Sid had another reprimand to add to his long list of "Reps."! The Sigm. on the same charge from our troop pleaded he'd had a TAB jab and got away with it so we're all pleased.

Episkopi, 4th May 1956

... We were told a story about the Naval Security when we went up to the TX Site last week. They are a bit scared of landing parties of EOKA Terrorists up there so when someone spotted a fishing boat at the beach one night the Navy was informed by radio 'phone from the site. "Right Ho, we'll send a destroyer" was the answer and about 25 minutes later a darkened shape glided round the headland

and a great beam of light suddenly shot across the bay to the fishing boat! A boat came across to investigate and you can just imagine the flap the fishermen were in!

Episkopi, 11th May 1956

... Big extra flaps lately with the hangings. We all laughed the other day, – we hear the Light Programme Radio Newsreel every night and the report from Nicosia said " there have been no reports of any Strikes in the rest of the island either".

It was still light here and we could see across to the building sites where work had been at a standstill all day. They are still off work today. In fact, with Greek Easter ending as the Strike began they've been off a week already.

Guards are heavier and so come round more frequently. We have now got the OK to go to the beach again but must go in groups and book in and out of the camp.

Episkopi, 23rd May 1956

... You will, by now, have heard of the mishap which occurred here yesterday when a Corporal was drowned. We don't know how much of the story will get into the papers at home.

He was Chris Cooper, the chap I sat next to on the 'plane from Egypt. He was a great friend of mine, we understood one another rather well as we were both somewhat odd in the same ways, we preferred to go out alone, we liked plants, we made solo trips to Jerusalem, and so on.

Chris went out alone yesterday morning for a swim. He was not a strong swimmer but liked to explore with a diving mask. When he didn't turn up for shift in the afternoon the other Cpl. thought he'd got a "drop shift" but asked about him at tea.

So someone from his tent came to ask if I'd seen him. They didn't like to report his absence for fear of getting him into trouble but I insisted that the Sgt. on his shift should be told, and he took charge and a search was made on the beaches.

When his clothes were found we all feared the worst, and his body was recovered from the water this morning. I feel particularly upset about him, he was always so active and interested. He earned the title of "Episkopi hair brain" though his eccentric doings were well known in Fayid too. He represented the Regt. in distance races in the Canal Zone, and did well.

Of course the Ceremonial Drill we have been doing on this Drill Course I'm on now has some point. The Drill Course is automatically chosen as the Firing Party and we will go as Guard of Honour to the funeral in Nicosia on Thursday.

Episkopi, Friday 25th May 1956

The funeral was yesterday, and we had quite a day. It was very nice to find your letter when I got back.

At 8 am when we Paraded for Drill we were told that the whole Ceremony must be perfected, in time to leave camp at 10.30 that morning for Nicosia, so we all had to put on any old KD to hand and rehearse like mad, learning a few new movements and perfecting the timing.

Then a frantic "Bull" session and we were loaded into a 3 ton truck to sit on folding wooden chairs for the two-hours-and-more drive across the island. Belts off but hats on at all times in the sweltering heat, with a warm breeze under the canvas rigged over our heads.

We arrived hot, weary, and somewhat dry, and had three quarters of an hour for lunch. A good (tinned) meal was laid on at the Nicosia Sqdn of the Regiment and the bods there were very obliging with their plates and irons.

Six full Cpls were with us for Bearer Party and the Nicosia Sqdn provided two more and a party of Mourners, to add to the truckload from here – most of Chris's shift had been allowed to come.

Then the Bearer Party left for the BMH and after an Inspection and final pep talk from the Q i/c our Squad, we got our three blanks and boarded the truck for the cemetery

The RSM, the Q, and the OC discussed the details. The CO chatted with the Padre, an RAF C of E one with a Scots accent, and the Volley Party (us) lined up at the end of the drive and "stood easy".

It was hot.

The Officers and other Mourners lined the drive. The wreaths were taken down to the grave-side. The Q pointed out our exact course and we waited and sweated, while the flies buzzed and tickled.

At last, some twenty minutes late, the coffin arrived and we heard the slow crunch of the tyres of the wagon crawling up the drive behind us as we stood in a double line at right angles to the drive.

A low word of Command, and the Volley Party crashed to Attention, Sloped, and Presented Arms as the hearse stopped – a low, cream, open truck, the flag-draped coffin flanked by the hatless Bearers sitting a little below it and facing it.

As they moved to take the weight of the coffin we Reversed Arms, Left Turned, and began a Slow March down the path, followed by the coffin and Mourners.

Some twenty five paces down, we Left Wheeled on to a wider path and Halted.

We turned inwards and Rested on the Arms Reversed – a movement in which first the rifle is brought from the left arm-pit to rest butt-upwards with the "spout" in the left boot toe. Then the right arm is shot to full extent to the right, and to a slow count of six, describes an arc to the front and snaps to the butt. Then the left arm repeats the process, the head following each arm in turn. Finally the elbows are dropped to the sides and the head drops forward. Fourteen people in unison make this a most solemn movement. As the heads dropped the coffin began to pass between our ranks, lovely timing.

The slow feet of the Bearers, then of the Officers, and finally the shaky feet of the Signalmen at the rear all passed through before we moved, Reversed Arms (into the armpit again) and turned to follow the last few yards, then, slowly between the Mourners and the grave, to stand across the foot of the grave, some four yards from it. Again we Rested on Arms Reversed and only by squinting through my eyebrows could I watch the Service, which began as soon as the RSM had removed the Flag, Hat and Belt.

The coffin was lowered gently into the grave and then the Padre began his Prayers and Readings. Near the foot, to the left, stood Mr. Hopkins, and Miss Chandler, two DSOs, to the right the OC and the CO. The Padre sprinkled earth and concluded his little Oration. My concentration slipped dangerously as I thought of Chris, but I recovered as we waited for the next Order, -"Volley Party, Present Arms", soft but crisp, in the hush of the hot afternoon.

We stooped over our rifles, paused for the usual 2 – 3 and crashed up into the "Present". Then we Sloped, and got the Order to Load. The rifles crashed to the Port, safety catches off, and the bolts cracked open as one. We fumbled in our belts for the first blank, shoved it home and at a whispered word, closed the bolts together in one clean smash. "Volley Party – Present" – and the rifles now whipped up to stand on the right shoulder, pointing slightly forward, the left hand hard in to the butt. "Volleys – Fire!"– "Volleys – Reload" and the rifles crashed down to the Port again.

The timing throughout was excellent, not one late bang or click. After three shots we Ordered Arms from the Port, then Fixed Bayonets, Sloped, and Presented.

With the final crash of this the Officers came to the Salute and the two R.E. Buglers sounded the Last Post. Finally, back to the Slope, and as the CO led the wreath laying party we Right Turned and marched off in Quick Time.

This morning we heard the CO thought the Drill "Perfect".

We got back here at 7.30 pm, stopping only for a lemonade on the way so you can imagine it was a tiring day.

Incidentally it was on the truck back that we heard from the Bearer Party of the reactions of the Cypriot bystanders as the hearse, with RMP Land Rover escort drove slowly from the BMH to the cemetery. Two elderly ladies were seen to rise to their feet. One old man removed his hat as they passed. The majority seemed rather amused at the sight – it must be quite common in Nicosia now that they have killed some 30 odd, and one man was seen to shake his fist and shout "Another one gone! Good!) Yesterday was "Empire Day".

The CO himself admired my garden this morning while I was out! First the SSM and the OC on their rounds sat chatting on my bed – (the others were off night shift and in bed). Then the CO came round with them on his inspection tour and stopped to chat with the OC when they came to my garden. They know my tent is clean and tidy so they don't chase me up on Inspection mornings. (Wish they could have seen my room at home!)

Episkopi, 28th May 1956

Well, these things never happen singly do they? Saturday, another accident occurred in the Regiment. Somebody had put a loaded (and I now hear, cocked) rifle in the room used as an Armoury up at the TX Site. The on-going Guard took the rifle and as he went out of the door pulled the trigger. The bullet hit a passing friend in the back about the waist and passing through his lung, came out through his chest.

The lad who fired the shot is now in BMH in a state of collapse and his Officer has stated quite definitely that he is not to be considered to blame – though the RMPs, who were called in at once were all for putting him in the Guard House immediately. They have only one cure for all mistakes – as if the mental shock etc. wasn't enough punishment. Once again it was the quiet, non-drinking type who died.

The island has had quite a weekend. Two RAF types drowned while bathing at Kyrenia; fatal injuries to Service people in a head-on bus crash; bombs thrown at Patrol vehicles in two places; Riots, in which Turks and Greeks fought and killed one another; and big forest fires fought by civvies and troops.

Saturday night some Commandos came in for a Dance here and I put two up in my tent as two beds are vacant. Sunday they showed me how to take a Browning automatic pistol to pieces and re-assemble it.

They told me they are all worried stiff as on Thursday they are to be marched through a town for a Queen's Birthday Parade, with empty rifles of course, and they don't expect to get away with it without some sort of EOKA action. Mad.

Episkopi, 14th June 1956

...Big fire in new building across the valley yesterday. Bomb in roof. The place was nearly finished. Made a nice drawing of the view this morning, stark black rafters – technique improved, cleaner colour.

Episkopi, 18th June 1956

I did the afternoon shift yesterday and missed a very busy night with urgent casualty messages about the twenty killed in the forest fire. Nasty business.

It's an odd sensation to be typing a tape listing casualties, next of kin and their addresses, and to know that when this tape finally reaches the War Office the awful news will be broken to the relatives listed. The tape ends with "NOK not informed" and the War Office does the informing, after which the names can be published.

... Did I tell you we had the Regimental Sports last Tuesday. Mr. Blair tried to raise a 1 Sqdn Team but support was very poor so I offered to make up the 220 relay team, though I can't run. Nor could the others so we were last!

... Have been encouraging a great model making craze in the camp. Planes and Galleons from kits sold by a Cypriot with a motor cycle and side car. I finished a 'plane for a bloke who got stuck, a little duration model – flies like a dream, he's highly chuffed (so am I).

Episkopi, 27th June 1956

Finished shift work last night for good, and here I am on my last Regimental Duty, RONCO for first and last time. (*Regimental Orderly Non Commissioned Officer*) Yesterday afternoon we had to attend an NCOs lecture on terrorist bombs and learnt a lot of things the papers don't print. Major Harrison, the "gen man" on the subject showed specimens and photos and told many stories. Most of the worst bombs are made from piping and the screw plugs used to make temporary stops when laying pipes.

Had an early night and reported, all dolled up in best KD and Puttees for the last time, collected bright red arm band and reported to the RSM. he said the Regt. was going down the drain and I was to pull up anyone I saw looking scruffy and, if needed, charge them. I said 'Yes Sir' every time he paused and at the end asked if I could report tomorrow in BD Shirt-sleeve Order as I'm on Release Kit Check -in other words – Blow the Regt. I'm going home! He said it would be OK and later got his own back by making me Escort to four cases on CO's Orders.

I have now seen the lot in the Army here, I've been to CO's even if not actually on them. I was marching in and out of that office 'till I almost joined in the cases!

They all got different results: First in – Out of Bounds in WRAC Compound, without Pay Book (RMP Charge) – 14 Days CB ; Second, just Out of Bounds in WRAC Compound – admonished; The third, handed in a Browning Pistol to the Armourer without checking it was not loaded, after a Sgt. had left it hurriedly in the Guard Room. It went off when the Armourer started fiddling. The Orderly Sgt charged the Armourer and the Armourer charged this chappie. He pleaded not knowing anything about that type of weapon and assuming the Sgt. would have checked – case dismissed (not the same as Admonished); the fourth, caught in bed, 2 hrs 40 minutes after Reveille, when he should have been on Works Parade – 7 days Pay stopped as he has a bad record of that sort of thing. The RSM later said in future he will see that the I/C of the tent gets charged, not the sleeper.

By this time we were late for dinner and I couldn't get much from the Cookhouse so I wasn't pleased. At tea time I wandered about the Cookhouse in the absence of the Ord. Sgt. and Ord. Officer but it was quite a decent meal so I won't be able to hand in a screed. Then I checked that all the Guards were present and correct (again no sign of Sgt. or Officer) and had my meal at second tea, and lasted it out until the fatigue party clearing bushes to reduce fire risk had about finished – the Sgt. had turned up and organised that.

Episkopi, 3rd July 1956

Herewith, almost for the sake of writing one, is the last letter I'll be sending from Episkopi. Before the Post tomorrow I'll be on my way to Nicosia. Today we sweated buckets and were interviewed (11 together) by the 2 I/C, as the Colonel was away. Then BD off again, and final packing done ready for an early start tomorrow.

Letters Home ~ 77

Nicosia Transit Camp, 6th July 1956

5 days to do and still here! We left Episkopi Wednesday morning with a promise of a flight Thursday. Hollow laughter when we got here as a lot of others had arrived on previous days with the same hopes. We had to report to Movements at 6 pm and when the Flight List for Thursday was read of course we weren't on it.

Six, including myself, were put down as Escorts for the next 24 hours and we had to stand by for any Escort Duties that were going. Not a bad job, riding in trucks and buses with a loaded rifle. Have seen a lot of Nicosia and area. One chap spent all day Thursday on a trip to Famagusta.

6 pm Thursday, the Friday list was read out, a short one as the 'plane was to carry a lot of Officers and WOs with families. Only four of the Signals party got on it so we put down to stay on Escort another day rather than go on fatigues like cookhouse cleaning and drainage trench digging in the baked earth. The 54 – 14 Release Group is due to be demobbed next Thursday, but there's still a lot here and they put a few 54 – 15s and even a 16 on flights in front of us. Causes some very hard feeling.

People continue to arrive, expecting a one night stop, and Officers and Sgts. etc continue to arrive and take the available seats. We escort them to their hotels and collect them in the morning.

Thursday being Pay Day we asked about money and drew £1 each at the most amusing Pay Parade I've ever attended. We sat in armchairs in a Naafi rest room and were paid by a keen Officer who returned all salutes and so added an extra comic twist as the men wore a variety of costumes from KD or BD shirt-sleeves to Denims or PT shorts and khaki shirts – hats being the only thing everyone wore and then they were all of different styles, colours and so on.

P.S. added at Nicosia Airport, 7th July 1956

Posting this after passing through Customs, etc at this end, now awaiting 'plane…

Packed and ready to go.